THE LANGUAGE OF EVALUATION

PURDUE UNIVERSITY MONOGRAPHS IN ROMANCE LANGUAGES

Volume 20

Louise Mirrer-Singer

The Language of Evaluation:
A Sociolinguistic Approach to the Story of
Pedro el Cruel in Ballad and Chronicle

LOUISE MIRRER–SINGER

THE LANGUAGE OF EVALUATION

A Sociolinguistic Approach to the Story of
Pedro el Cruel in Ballad and Chronicle

JOHN BENJAMINS PUBLISHING COMPANY
Amsterdam/Philadelphia

1986

Library of Congress Cataloging in Publication Data

Mirrer-Singer, Louise
　The language of evaluation.

　(Purdue University monographs in Romance languages, ISSN 0165-8743; v. 20)
　Bibliography: p.
　1. Pedro I., King of Castile and Leon, 1334-1369, in fiction, drama, poetry, etc. 2. Spanish literature -- To 1500 -- History and criticism. 3. Romancero del rey don Pedro. 4. López de Ayala, Pedro, 1332-1407. Coronica del rey don Pedro. I. Title. II. Series.
　PQ6049.P33M57　　　　1986　　　860'.9'351　　86-9620
　ISBN 90 272 1730 0 (European) / ISBN 0-915027-69-0 (US) (alk. paper)

To Philip

Contents

List of Tables

Acknowledgments

I should like to thank the following teachers and friends who gave me invaluable criticism and encouragement during the various stages of this study: Rina Benmayor, to whom I owe a particular debt of gratitude; Jean Franco, David Halle, Helen Nader, Kathleen Newman, and Mary Pratt; and Louis Singer, who read the manuscript in its earliest period of development and offered many thoughtful comments. I should also like to thank Samuel G. Armistead, who, from the time I was an undergraduate student of his at the University of Pennsylvania to the present, has served as a mentor and an inspiration in the field of medieval Spanish literature. Stanford University and the Whiting Foundation afforded me generous grants which gave me the opportunity to explore the various issues touched on in this work.

Abbreviations

AEM	*Anuario de Estudios Medievales*
BAE	Biblioteca de Autores Españoles
BH	*Bulletin Hispanique*
BHS	*Bulletin of Hispanic Studies*
ExTL	*Explicación de Textos Literarios*
HR	*Hispanic Review*
JAF	*Journal of American Folklore*
JMRS	*Journal of Medieval and Renaissance Studies*
MLN	*Modern Language Notes*
MLR	*Modern Language Review*
NBAE	Nueva Biblioteca de Autores Españoles
NLH	*New Literary History*
NRF	*Nouvelle Revue Française*
NRFH	*Nueva Revista de Filología Hispánica*
RCEH	*Revista Canadiense de Estudios Hispánicos*
RFE	*Revista de Filología Española*
RN	*Romance Notes*
RPh	*Romance Philology*
RH: Historia	*El romancero hoy: Historia, comparatismo, biblio-grafía crítica.* Ed. Samuel G. Armistead et al. Madrid: C.S.M.P., 1979.
RH: Poética	*El romancero hoy: Poética.* Ed. Diego Catalán et al. Madrid: C.S.M.P., 1979.
SP	*Studies in Philology*
WF	*Western Folklore*

1

Introduction

¿Qué pide María de Padilla,   qué pide por aguinaldo?
La cabeza del Maestro,   del rey don Pedro su hermano.[1]

These verses, sung today as part of a *canto aguinaldero* in the Spanish provinces of Segovia and Zamora, belong to an oral tradition that dates back to the Middle Ages. The lines refer to the years of political turmoil and bloodshed that marked the reign of Pedro I, King of Castile. The question and answer they present recollect the bitter hatred between the Castilian monarch and his illegitimate half brothers, the Trastámaras. Invoking the name of the King's mistress, María de Padilla, they also recall the strained relations between Pedro and his wife, doña Blanca de Borbón.

Clearly, the context within which the present-day *canto aguinaldero* is sung differs radically from that of the fourteenth-century *romance* it brings to mind.[2] Yet the fact that the verses continue to detail the mistress's savage demand for the head of the King's half brother indicates that the Spanish *Romancero* is a vital tradition capable of at once supporting the poetic and ideological legacy of the Middle Ages and the preoccupations of contemporary life.[3]

The Spanish *Romancero* is described by Diego Catalán as

> poesía oral de creación colectiva, capaz de retener, durante siglos y siglos, memoria fiel de toda una serie de pormenores tocantes a un suceso pretérito, real o imaginario, pero, a la vez, abierta a continua renovación, a continua re-creación.[4]

It has at its base an oral literary form which is maximally accessible to a general public. The *Romancero* language is virtually free of the figurative speech common to lyric poetry. Its preponderance of verbs and nouns lends it "a certain forthrightness,"[5] and its direct manner, seen in the extensive use of the vocative,[6] affords a wide appeal. But the properties of the *Romancero* that have allowed infinite recasting of the *romances* go beyond this formal base. On the one hand, it is the tradition of anonymity in the collective re-creation of the

1

texts which invests the *Romancero* with its distinctive *apertura*.[7] On the other, it is the stories contained in the *romances* and the way in which they are narrated that have advanced the *Romancero* as an open-ended genre.

The story content of a particular *romance* is often a key element in its longevity, for the open-ended nature of narrative is its capacity to be reinterpreted so that one story spawns another. Some stories, which feature historical or political situations, seem to have a natural capability for inspiring public interest beyond the actual events they relate. These stories convert specific historical events into philosophical abstractions which are of general "human interest" and, therefore, are forever relevant.

The timeless qualities of these types of stories have not gone unnoticed in *Romancero* studies. Menéndez Pidal, for example, addresses this topic in his examination of the *romances noticieros,* concluding that many of these "news-bearing" ballads have perished because "los romances noticieros sólo perduran cuando les sostiene su propio valor intrínseco o el interés general de una época memorable."[8]

The verses cited at the beginning of this chapter exemplify the life-prolonging traits Menéndez Pidal points to. They undoubtedly were prompted by the *noticiero Romance de don Fadrique*, yet because they conserve nothing of the historical context within which they originated, their survival must be attributed to more than lasting historical interest alone. Figuring significantly in the timelessness of these lines is the quality of *tellability*, or *reportability*. The shocking demand for a human head made through the two verses of the *canto aguinaldero* would occupy under any circumstances a high place on the "unspoken permanent agenda" of reportable matters.[9] The story of María de Padilla's bloodthirstiness concerns a flagrant violation of customary rules of behavior, worthy of introduction into any number of narrative or dramatic situations.[10] The same is true of many other long-enduring *romances* and *romance* fragments, including additional, related *romances noticieros* from the *Romancero del rey don Pedro* that have found themselves incorporated into dissociated plays and histories.[11] An additional reason for survival has to do with the form in which the content is cast. The *canto aguinaldero,* for example, is a traditional Christmas song which is performed each winter as part of the season's festivities.

There is, however, another important factor in the *tellability* of even the most extraordinary stories. It is possible to tell the same story in different ways, making different points, or sometimes, no point at all. Because a point-less story obscures the reportability of the events it describes, a skilled narrator makes use of grammatical devices to aid in directing audience attention to the story's *raison d'être.* For example, the two verses from the *canto aguinaldero* cited above use a question-and-answer format rather than an "objective" third person narration to present María de Padilla's Christmas wish. The consequence of this syntactic maneuver is to foreground María's outrageous response to a conventional question. The events of the medieval *romance noticiero*—i.e., María's request for Fadrique's head—are thus made relevant to their new form. The interrogative framework of the verses in the *canto aguinaldero* points to the worthiness of the story for report. It says, in effect, that somebody broke the normal rules in a shocking—and reportable—way.

The above example demonstrates that the capacity of a story to outlive its original context through telling and retelling may be largely contingent upon the storytellers who appropriate it. These storytellers are constrained to narrate their stories in ways that will attract and hold the attention of an audience with whom they are in a face-to-face situation. Recent experiments in story recall also show that the way in which a story is told can be essential to its retention by an audience.[12] These experiments have demonstrated that a story which concerns an unusual event, but which is related in an unmemorable manner, will be met by an unenthusiastic audience unlikely to preserve it.

The idea that both structure and content play an important role in the persistence of the *Romancero* tradition has been taken up in various quarters. The theories of formulistic diction in *Romancero* composition[13] and underlying "deep structures"[14] in the ballad corpus are two important endeavors in this direction. But as the *canto aguinaldero* verses indicate, the durability of the *Romancero* may have something to do also with the surface level linguistic devices used by singers to impress upon their audience the point of the story in the *romance*. One area that takes up this issue is sociolinguistics.

William Labov, a sociolinguist who has studied the relationship of grammatical structures in a narrative to the tellability of its story,[15] has proposed that the syntactic complexities found in a text indicate the narrative's very reason for being, or the narrator's rationale in recounting it (Labov 366).

Labov points to four major headings in his investigations under which these elements, which he calls *evaluative devices,* may be classified. They are the intensifiers, the comparators, the correlatives, and the explicatives. Intensifiers are evaluative devices that single out a particular event in the narrative and strengthen it by means of gestures, repetition, quantifiers, and ritual utterance. Comparators—which include negative, future, interrogative, and imperative clauses—contrast events in the narrative that actually occurred with those that did not. Correlatives consist of clauses that join two or more events in the narrative—often through verbal tense manipulations. Finally, explicatives interpret particular actions or situations through causal and conjunctive expressions (Labov 378-93).

Evaluative devices are used in the narrative to capture and maintain audience interest, as well as to make clear the point of a story's content. These devices thus may be related to both the artistic intent of a narrator and to the problem of rhetorically engaging audience sympathy for the underlying message of a text.[16] These properties are particularly important to the *Romancero* tradition, and the singers of the *romances* regularly incorporate evaluative devices into their compositions both to maintain audience interest and to establish the group dynamic so vital to the *Romancero* tradition. The transmitters of the *romances* similarly use linguistic strategies to rework their texts within different social, historical, and geographical structures. Their success in this venture is reflected in the very *tradicionalidad* of the ballad.

The concept of evaluation in the *romances* becomes perhaps most crucial when one turns to the study of the *romances noticieros,* recalled by such lines as the verses from the *canto aguinaldero* cited above. The *noticieros* were composed for their particular historical moment, but because the essence of these *romances* was their news-spreading function, it was necessary for the singers who transmitted them to "market" the stories they contained. Evaluative devices, which indicate to an audience that the events involved in a particular narrative are worthy of report, helped significantly in this project. However, some of the *romances noticieros* served also as vehicles for political propaganda.[17] Because evaluative devices direct attention to the point of a story, they could be used by singers to elaborate a partisan view. The skillful handling of evaluative devices (negative and interrogative constructions; future, conditional, and imperfect verb forms; dialogue, etc.) in these texts led to a subtle registering of ideological points in what has been termed the *guerra civil romancística* of the late Middle Ages.[18]

In light of the proposed connection between evaluative devices and the *production* and *reproduction* of the *romances,* the texts chosen for detailed consideration in this study are compositions that clearly reflect both the complex syntactic maneuvers discussed above and the social and historical structures of the period in which they were produced and transmitted. Six *romances* from the *Romancero del rey don Pedro* will be discussed in great detail. These compositions have been chosen as illustrations of evaluation in the *Romancero* because the concentration of evaluative devices found in their verses forms a direct response to the poetic and ideological requirements of their singers and audiences.

The Pedro cycle consists of a group of *romances noticieros* that detail the hostilities between King Pedro I of Castile and his bastard brothers, the Trastámaras. The *romances* were probably composed during the fourteenth century by *juglares* in the service of the respective factions. Their purpose would have been both to spread slander and innuendo against the members of the opposing parties and to legitimize the violent overthrow of the legal heir to the Castilian throne when the Trastámarans came to power. The *romances* were also recalled in a powerful Castilian family's claim for "pure" and royal blood, and eventually, they became identified with the concepts of cruel and inhumane rule by an unjust king which they presented.[19]

The texts to be discussed in this study are representative of the various stages in the production and reproduction of the *Romancero del rey don Pedro.* They include two versions of the *Romance de la muerte de doña Blanca* that tell of Pedro's malevolent behavior towards his wife;[20] two versions of the *Romance del rey don Pedro* that describe the King's refusal to heed God's warnings and to return Castile to just rule;[21] and two versions of the *Romance de doña Blanca*—one which lobbies for the reinstatement of Pedro's family,[22] and another which supports the Almirante de Castilla family's claim for "pure" and royal blood[23]—that suggest an adulterous affair between the King's wife and his half brother.

The texts of the *Romancero del rey don Pedro* are particularly instructive illustrations of evaluation in the narrative because they make use of a wide variety of complex syntactic structures in order to convey their ideas. Verbal tense maneuvers, for example, elsewhere noted as a remarkable feature of *Romancero* grammar,[24] can be seen in the Pedro cycle as evaluating for the audience the disorder of fourteenth-century Castilian political events. Other linguistic strategies similarly interpret and reformulate the activities of the turbulent period, in some cases so masterfully that the ideological principles they promoted came to define new conditions for monarchal succession in Castile.[25]

The impact of such far-reaching evaluative strategies as are found in the *Romancero del rey don Pedro* is felt most forcefully when one turns to the medieval chronicles, which sometimes used the evaluative properties of the *Romancero* structures to reshape the *romances* into the authoritative molds of historical discourse. This phenomenon forms a unique demonstration of the re-creative abilities of the *Romancero*. The integration of the *Romancero del rey don Pedro* into Pero López de Ayala's *Crónica del rey don Pedro* is one such example. In this chronicle, the language of the *romances* functions to enhance the authorial point of view.

The discussion of the language of evaluation in the *Romancero* will unfold during the course of this study in the following manner:

Chapter 2 will provide an outline of the various explanations that have been proposed in traditional *Romancero* criticism for the type of linguistic structures characteristically found in the *romances*. It will also suggest a critique of these explanations based on their failure to adequately consider the relation between the *Romancero* grammar and the historical and social situation within which the *romances* are performed.

Chapter 3 will elaborate on this critique in the proposal of a sociolinguistic approach to the *romances*. This type of approach considers the grammatical features of the *Romancero* as evaluative devices and links their use in the *romances* to the intentions of singers in performing their compositions, and to the attitudes and beliefs of the audience which attends them.

Chapter 4 will specifically address the issue of evaluation in the *Romancero* through a detailed study of six texts from the *Romancero del rey don Pedro*. These texts have been the subject of surprisingly few studies, and those critics who have considered them have done so largely by reflecting only on their ideas and not on their structures.[26] This study argues that both the information presented in the texts and their grammatical arrangements reflect the relationship between the *romances* and historical parameters. Furthermore, it proposes a sociolinguistic approach as a methodology which allows a better understanding of the connection between the language of the Pedro texts and their historical and social framework.

Chapter 5 of this study will introduce the *Crónica del rey don Pedro* as an example of the ideological impact of evaluation in the *romances* when they are recast within the context of an historical work. The subject of the *romances* as source material for some of the medieval chronicles is interesting in terms of the study of the language of evaluation, for some chroniclers relied heavily on the *Romancero* for adding both content and structure to their historical works. As Menéndez Pidal has commented:

> a ellos [los romances] volvieron la vista los historiadores, habituados a contar siempre con los relatos poéticos que los juglares cantaban "ad recreationem et forte ad informationem."[27]

The texts of the *Romancero del rey don Pedro* that were incorporated into Pero López de Ayala's *Crónica del rey don Pedro* functioned in precisely this manner, and the examination of the *romances* in the chronicle leads to a provocative reassessment of the open-ended nature of the *Romancero*.

Chapter 6 will propose certain conclusions which arise from the study. In brief, it will suggest that the effectiveness of evaluative devices in composition and transmission is particularly evident in the *romances noticieros,* which played an important role in the sociopolitical mission of the state and its opponents during the late Middle Ages. But it will also note that the linguistic mechanisms singers use in telling their stories most effectively and memorably are not unique to this group of *romances.* Rather, it is through syntactic and lexical maneuvers—within respective historical, geographical, and social situations—that the "deep structures" of all the *romances* are transformed into their surface level incarnations.

In sum, this study will seek to demonstrate that throughout centuries of re-creation, linguistic devices have been used to support both the production and the reproduction of the *romances.* On the basis of this demonstration, it will be argued that it is time to recognize these devices as evaluators and to include a discussion of evaluative mechanisms in the study of the *Romancero* tradition.

The Language of the *Romancero*

A. *Romancero* Grammar

Critics have for some time discussed the remarkable characteristics of *Romancero* "grammar." This is because the language of the *romances* makes unusual recourse to a wide variety of syntactic and lexical items, including a distinctive use of tense and aspect,[1] ritual utterances, and languages other than Spanish. The following text from the fifteenth-century *Romancero* provides a striking demonstration of this characteristic patterning of *Romancero* language:

Romance de la morilla burlada

	a	b
1	Yo me era mora Moraima,	morilla de un bel catar;
2	cristiano vino a mi puerta,	cuitada, por me engañar;
3	hablóme en algarabía	como aquél que la bien sabe:
4	— ¡Ábraseme las puertas, mora,	si Alá te guarde de mal! —
5	— ¿Cómo te abriré, mezquina,	que no sé quién te serás? —
6	— Yo soy el moro Mazote,	hermano de la tu madre;
7	que un cristiano dejo muerto,	tras mí venía el alcalde;
8	si no me abres tú, mi vida,	aquí me verás matar. —
9	Cuando esto oí, cuitada,	comencéme a levantar;
10	vistiérame una almejía	no hallando mi brial,
11	fuérame para la puerta	y abríla de par en par.[2]

The *Romance de la morilla burlada* is a work which relies heavily on linguistic maneuvering for its impact. It employs seven different verbal tenses and aspects in its composition: the present, the imperfect, the present subjunctive, the imperative, the future, the preterite, and the archaic *-ra* form.[3] The use of these different verbal tenses and aspects presents a deviance from the standard narrative tenses—i.e., the preterite or, in some specialized cases, the imperfect[4]—that might otherwise be expected in the simple relation of the story. These different verbal forms also—along with negative, imperative, interrogative, and other equally "complex" clauses found in the *romance*— deviate from what may be termed a "basic narrative syntax"[5] in which the verbal sequence of clauses matches the sequence of events described.

Basic narrative syntax is an important concept in the study of the characteristic patterning of *Romancero* language. It refers to the type of structures found in the sequential recapitulation of past events and consists essentially in a series of eight elements without a hierarchical phrase structure.[6] These elements are: (1) the sentence adverbial, (2) the subject noun phrase, and (3) to (8) the verb phrase. These eight elements are more fully described in the outline below:

(1) conjunctions, including temporals, *pues, y, luego*;
(2) simple subjects: pronouns, proper names, *mi hermana, esa muchacha*;
(3) the underlying auxiliary, a simple past tense marker which is incorporated (generally) into the verb;
(4) preterite verbs, with adverbial particles;
(5) complements of varying complexity: direct and indirect objects;
(6) manner or instrumental adverbs;
(7) locative adverbials;
(8) temporal adverbials and comitative clauses.[7]

When one understands how simple basic narrative syntax is, it is easier to show the effect of syntactic complexities in a narrative when they do occur. In the *Romance de la morilla burlada,* for example, basic narrative syntax is transgressed at the very moments in the text when specific events, details, or attitudes that call attention to the story's *raison d'être* are described.[8] The dialogue section of the *romance* is one such instance. In this part of the work, the preterite tense is abruptly abandoned for the present form. The result is a suspension of the action of the narrative with a concomitant "focusing-in" on the protagonists of the *romance* who "speak for themselves."

The verbal tense maneuvers found in dialogue sections of a large number of *romances* are typical infractions of basic narrative syntax in the *Romancero.* Not only is there a switch from the standard narrative tenses to, generally, the present in these sections, but often there is an unexpected introduction of the imperfect form as well. Illustrative of this point is the line "tras mí venía el alcalde" (7b) in the *Romance de la morilla burlada.* This mixing of tense and aspect has, as will later be shown, become one of the most troublesome issues in *Romancero* grammar criticism.

The syntactic devices detailed above are not the only media through which a characteristic patterning of *Romancero* language may be seen. The *romances* typically make use also of distinctive words and phrases that similarly call attention to situations in the narrative that are in some way peculiar or exceptional. The recourse to a foreign language (forty percent of the nouns in the composition are of Arabic origin[9]) and to ritual utterance in the *Romance de la morilla burlada* are representative. The following sections of this study will show that these lexical constructions, along with the various syntactic devices, function in the *Romancero* to evaluate and interpret for the audience the details of the events recapitulated through the verses of the *romances*.

As the above discussion of complexities in the *Romance de la morilla burlada* suggests, there are certain regularities that occur in *Romancero* language, and these regularities may be connected with the kind of activity that prevails in *Romancero* composition and transmission. The precise qualification of this connection, however, has been difficult to establish. The resultant division of opinion among *Romancero* critics is the subject of the remaining sections of this chapter.

Briefly, the problem has been that critics disagree in principle on the nature of *Romancero* production and reproduction. As a consequence, the proposals they have put forth to account for the *Romancero* grammar reflect a wide variety of theories. Concentrating largely on the verbal tense system of the ballads—presumably because they view this system as the most outstanding characteristic of *Romancero* language—different critics have pointed in their studies to artistic intent, contamination between compositions, musical modulations, rhyme scheme, metrics, and careless orthography as possible forces behind the varying tenses. It is significant, however, that the nature of the oral literary situation which gives rise to the *Romancero* language has been addressed only in the vaguest of terms by these critics, and even then without reference to actual performance, past or present, of the *romances*.

The present chapter attempts to describe some of the more salient features of *Romancero* grammar criticism. The critical issue, however, is whether any one explanation will prove sufficient to cover all of the distinctive elements contained in the language of the *romances*. The picture which slowly emerges as a result of the study at hand portrays the *Romancero* as a complex and multi-dimensioned creation, and it seems that a theory which claims to explain the linguistic characteristics discussed in this chapter must present a more synthetic approach to the ballad materials. For these reasons, sociolinguistics will later be suggested as a point of departure.

B. *Une beauté grammaticale*:
The Stylistic Approach to Language in the *Romancero*

In a well-known article on the "style" of Flaubert, Marcel Proust refers to the manipulation of language in the works of the nineteenth-century novelist as "une beauté grammaticale." What Proust meant by this term was that Flaubert, whose syntax was such that "un bon élève, chargé de relire [s]es épreuves . . . eût été capable d'en effacer bien des fautes,"[10] used grammar in an unusual way to effect an impression on his audience. Specifically, Flaubert arrived at what Proust calls "l'étroite, l'hermétique continuité du style" (74) by including in his sentences syntactic usages that lay outside of the rules of grammar: pronouns that did not correspond to the people to whom they logically referred; rule-bending placement of adverbs in the middle and at the end of sentences; the conjunction *et,* "[qui] n'a nullement dans Flaubert l'objet que la grammaire lui assigne" (78); and a use of tense and aspect, in particular, the imperfect, in a manner that changed entirely "l'aspect des choses et des êtres, comme font une lampe qu'on a déplacée" (78).

Proust's discussion of language and style in Flaubert is a familiar one in the realm of epic and ballad criticism.[11] Proust characterized Flaubert as

Un homme qui par l'usage entièrement nouveau et personnel qu'il a fait du passé défini, du passé indéfini, du participe présent, de certains pronoms et de certaines prépositions, a renouvelé . . . notre vision des choses. (72)

He went on to conclude of Flaubert's language that

Ces singularités grammaticales traduisant en effet une vision nouvelle, que d'application ne fallait-il pas pour bien fixer cette vision pour la faire passer de l'inconscient dans le conscient, pour l'incorporer enfin aux diverses parties du discours. (80)

In so doing Proust unwittingly established many of the terms that are now used to discuss the epic and ballad literature of the Middle Ages.

Flaubert was not, as Proust believed, the first to manipulate syntax for stylistic effect. The "unique" grammar of Romance oral literature predates Flaubert's syntactic deviances by several centuries. Long before Flaubert's "emploi nouveau des temps des verbes," the composer of the *Chanson de Roland* alternated present with past and perfect tenses to achieve the changes of aspect, dramatic intensity, and other nontemporal effects of language[12] thought by Proust to be original with Flaubert. As regards the use of the imperfect, the Spanish *Romancero* provides a plethora of examples of what has similarly been termed a stylistic employment of verb morphemes. However, while Proust may have been wrong about the novelty of his subject's style, he nevertheless pointed out to critics examining the literature of a previous era, in which grammar was similarly employed, what are now key elements in the stylistic approach to language in the epic and ballad. The question of why grammar is used in literature in ways that seem uncharacteristic of ordinary speech therefore is both current and historical, and Proust's answer for the nineteenth-century Flaubert is important to understand because it has been perhaps equally as influential in shaping the terms used to discuss *Romancero* grammar as it has been in Flaubert criticism.

In his article, Proust directs much attention to his subject's use of the imperfect to attain a unique effect. He comments, "cet imparfait sert à rapporter non seulement, les paroles mais toute la vie des gens" (78). The use of the imperfect has similarly provoked the greatest interest from oral literature critics, and many of them use Proust's language to describe its effect. Both Stephen Gilman and Joseph Szertics speak of the imperfect as qualifying the character of life, as seen through the narrative. Gilman writes of the imperfect:

> Su carácter incompleto, resaltado y valorado (como expresión de acción en proceso) frente al normal carácter incompleto del presente modifica la visión narrativa.[13]

Szertics remarks:

> el imperfecto sirve muy bien para reproducir estados de ánimo y toda la vida interior de los personajes, esto es, "la durée humaine" bergsoniana. (104)

But the stylistic use of the imperfect must be seen within the context of the entire question of verb morphemes in the Romance languages.

William Bull, in *Time, Tense, and the Verb,* argues that in general verb morphemes in the Spanish language deal with eight items of information: lexical meaning, verb class, aspect, order relations, axes of orientation, mode, person, and number.[14] However, as Bull rightly suggests, there are exceptions to this rule. The imperfect, for example, indicated in Spanish by the morphemes *ía* and *aba*, by no means provides in every case a clear indication of all eight items of information. In fact, in terms of the epic and ballad, the imperfect form often makes a contribution to meaning which is far from obvious. The problem is that the imperfect, although physically differentiated from other verbal forms by a distinctive morpheme, has, within the context of an actual composition, an uncertain grammatical distinction. This is perhaps a general problem with verbal tense and aspect within epic and ballad literature as a whole. This is because, as Proust has noted, it is sometimes the case that grammatical items are assigned by their patrons functions that would otherwise be discouraged by the rules of grammar. This topic lies at the very base of the stylistic approach to language in Romance oral literature: when verbal tense and aspect are alternated as frequently as they are in some epics and ballads, the proponents of this approach look to stylistics for an explanation.

C. "Altos son y relucían"

The stylistic approach, as outlined by Proust and many *Romancero* critics, presumes a manipulation of ordinary speech by a writer or, in the case of oral literature, by a singer, to produce certain artistic effects. Proust has claimed that Flaubert's manipulations have the effect of an arc, springing from the precise center of one proposition and landing the reader in the very heart of the next. Gilman suggests that, in the *Poema del Cid,* the mixture of tenses—"un fenómeno de estilo"—makes "individual poetic contributions" (*Tiempo* 24) to the temporal unity of the text and produces the effect which the audience understands as the "objectivity" of the epic. Other critics have considered such stylistic effects as the mobility of the narrative point of view, the enlivening of the narrative, and the avoidance of monotony by varying verbal tense. However, a problem of this stylistic approach to a phenomenon such as the mixture of verb forms in a composition is that not all critics will agree on the nature of the effects of this mixture in any given text. A clear example of the consequences for critics who see style as a governing force in the manipulation of language by a singer is the polemic resulting from stylistic criticism of the well-known *Romance de Abenámar.* One of the outstanding features of this *romance* is the mixture of tense and aspect found in a line such as the title of this section, "Altos son y relucían."

Leo Spitzer, a critic who was preoccupied throughout his career with the stylistic employment of the imperfect in epic and ballad poetry, argues that in the *Romance de Abenámar* the transformation of present actions to actions performed in the past—indicated by the line "altos son y relucían," as well as "el Alhambra era, Señor" and "el moro que a mí me tiene   muy grande bien me quería"—demonstrates the exigencies of *cortesía* in the transaction between King Juan II and Abenámar, the two *dramatis personae* of the *romance.* Spitzer writes, "Así los imperfectos sugieren que la conversación continúa en un nivel de cortesía."[15] But Spitzer also recognizes the prevalence of the -*ía* assonant rhyme scheme in the ballads as contributing to the stylistic value of the imperfect tense. Here the use of the imperfect harks not to a qualitative analysis of the tone of a *romance* but rather to the quantitative effect of the accumulation of like sounds at the end of rhymed lines. Spitzer asks:

¿Cuál es en efecto el valor estilístico de la tirada asonantada monorrima del romance? ¿No es el de una tensión contínua, de un martilleo monótono que nos hace esperar con ansia un aflojamiento, una relajación—y que en efecto, en la mayoría de los romances, termina en una explosión epigramática o un efecto final como un estallido? (22)

The point is that there is an artistic use of time—not just tense—in the ballads:

> En el lapso . . . más breve posible el romance debe desarrollar sus efectos, hipnotizarnos y despertarnos, trasportarnos a un clima histórico y producir una impresión supratemporal, darnos un todo y dejarnos perplejos ante lo fragmentario de la vida, evocar el drama de la vida y a la vez resolverlo en un contenido intelectual epigramático. El harpa eólica del poeta popular se transforma aquí en un reloj que con su tictac riguroso escande el tiempo, lo cronometra, y la terminación de la unidad de tiempo que en el romance es señalada como por la brusca llamada de un despertador. (22)

Spitzer's conclusions, particularly those concerning courtesy as a motive for the use of the imperfect in the *Romance de Abenámar,* have been both implicitly and explicitly challenged in the works of other stylistic critics. Karl Vossler, for example, presented this view in the "Carta española a Hugo von Hofmannsthal":

> Con el "relucían" en la voz del rey Don Juan y con el "era" de las palabras del moro Abenámar se introdujera, al mismo tiempo, la voz del poeta que quiere estar allí presente, o, visto por otro lado, como si el rey y el moro quisieran prolongar y hacer llegar hasta nosotros sus propósitos.[16]

Joseph Szertics's analysis attributes "una función desrealizadora" to the use of the imperfect in *Abenámar.* He writes:

> El romance empieza en un ambiente de ensueño y por medio del imperfecto la visión de Granada se nos aparece más fantástica, a la vez que las palabras de los dos interlocutores adquieren matices imaginarios. . . . El ambiente inicial de ensueño se prolonga merced a la alternancia "presente-imperfecto"—son y relucían—en la pregunta del rey y viene reforzado todavía más por "era" en la respuesta de Abenámar. (72-73)

Szertics's view is in general shared by Menéndez Pidal in the *Romancero hispánico*:

> Los cambios más violentos realizados en el romance no son sino huída de la pesada, insoportable, lógica narrativa, gusto de lo inmotivado, lo misterioso, lo fantástico. A cierta irrealidad de expresión se pueden atribuir algunas de las mayores singularidades sintácticas que se hallan en el romancero, por ejemplo en el uso de los tiempos verbales.[17]

The discussion of the stylistic use of verbal tense not only in the ballad *Abenámar,* but in all Romance epic and ballad literature, continues almost *ad infinitum.* Perhaps this is because the stylistic approach invites each critic to use impressionistic, rather than purely linguistic, criteria in examining the literature. This is attractive in that the epic and the ballads themselves seem to overstep the conventional boundaries of linguistics and, as will be shown in later sections, make use of features that have traditionally been considered extralinguistic.[18] Nevertheless, the stylistic approach has its detractors.

D. The Assonance Argument

Excluding such arguments as poetic ineptitude or "libre sintáxis popular" as motivations for the peculiar *Romancero* grammar, the most powerful criticism of the stylistic approach comes from those who contend that the syntax in the *romances* results from prosodic restrictions and has little to do with artistic intent.[19]

The principal requisite of the *Romancero* form is an assonant rhyme scheme. Since the ballads rely heavily on verb forms to meet the requirements of this scheme, some critics have theorized that the choice of verb forms and their arrangement within a given ballad are simply a consequence of the assonance pattern. Manfred Sandmann, for example, has argued that in the *Romancero* the prosodic principle dominates over grammatical demands, and that verb forms are often employed "para llenar un verso y para disponer de una rima conveniente."[20]

Ballad critics have in general been quick to point out the correlation between the poetic form of the *romances* and their syntactic constructions. However, most have argued against assonance as the single determining factor in the unusual *Romancero* grammar. This is because the order of influence in questions of form and content is far from clear. Spitzer, for example, has argued that the form of the *romances* was originally shaped by questions more universal than rhyme scheme. In his article on the *Romance de Conde Arnaldos* he writes, "Is not the dialogue of Man with Nature (or Fate) an eternal theme in popular poetry and may it not even be that this thematic dialogue may explain the dialogue form of the romances?"[21] In the article cited earlier, Spitzer argues that the pre-established scheme of the *romances* provides a common vehicle for the different ballad themes—"la música del mar del mundo" (29). Other critics have been reluctant to lend much weight to the assonance argument because it detracts from the poetic statement made by the *Romancero*. Szertics, for example, writes:

La rima y el metro son sólo medios, pero de ningún modo el fin de la creación poética. A nuestro entender, la mayor parte de las irregularidades temporales que se puedan observar en el *Romancero Viejo* pueden explicarse, ante todo, por razones estilísticas. (15)

Moreover, it must be remarked that peculiarities of the *Romancero* grammar go beyond questions of verbal tense and the assonance of certain verb forms. The choice of certain lexical items in a ballad, for example, can hardly be shown to conform simply to assonance patterns. Remembering that the Spanish verb morpheme reflects such information as person and number, it can be seen that lexis is an important consideration in the discussion of the shape of verb forms. One does not find, for example, liberties taken in the *Romancero* with subject-verb agreement for the sake of assonance. It is easy to imagine a rule making assonance easier to fabricate—the admittance into poetry, for instance, of the form *él hablo* as well as *yo hablo* would certainly make assonance easier—yet as this is never the case, it is clear that there must be additional reasons for the allowance of tense-aspect manipulation. In short, the interests of an assonant rhyme scheme may well cause certain verb forms to be rejected as others are included (e.g., "altos son y relucían," rather than *relucen*). However, the constraints imposed by lexical items must be weighed at least equally when dealing with syntactic restrictions in the *Romancero* (e.g., "altos son y relucían," but never *relucimos*).

E. *Architecture temporelle*

An argument which at once supports stylistic criticism and points out the limitations of purely artistic considerations in approaching the *Romancero* grammar comes from French critics such as Jean-Claude Chevalier ("Architecture temporelle du 'Romancero tradicional'"[22]) and Michèle Débax ("La problématique du narrateur dans le 'Romancero tradicional'"[23]). *Architecture temporelle,* the term used to refer to the approach these critics take, regards verbal tense as having a *thetic* value within the narrative (Chevalier 65). In other words, tenses are not manipulated for artistic effect alone, but more importantly are used to position an audience within and outside of the ballad being sung. The principal element in this type of criticism is the relationship between the narrator of a ballad and its recipients. The narrator holds a single point of view and uses language to move the audience not simply emotionally, as Menéndez Pidal proposes, but quite literally, from one time period (*stase*) to the next. In this manner, the narrator constantly reminds the auditors of their own position in time, for verbal tense does not just function as a means of drawing attention to particular characters, providing dramatic intensity or other stylistic effects; it relates directly to the temporal order of the "outside world." The present tense is the present of the audience. The singer, by using this tense, projects the listeners into the very unfolding of the facts being reported simultaneously in the ballad. The preterite tense effects a translation of ballad time into "real" time. The imperfect becomes a vehicle for transporting the audience to the precise moment in the ballad during which an action takes place. The combination of verbal tense and aspect in the *Romancero* thus provides the singer with a means of leading the audience (Chevalier says, "Il le chauffe") through the ballad. As Chevalier writes, "il l'en écarte, il le met à distance, il modère les élans qu'il a provoqués et qu'il ravive l'instant d'après" (65). A new definition of the ballad thus arises: a *romance* is "l'inscription dans un mouvement général d'unités fixes où se déploient à leur tour des mouvements internes" (64).

Chevalier, the chief proponent of *architecture temporelle,* admits into his argument the impressions of the stylistic critics (85). Indeed, *architecture temporelle* incorporates many of the "intuitions" of Menéndez Pidal, Szertics, and others, and Chevalier in fact uses the word "stylistic" (although he calls it a "dangerous" word) in his account of the use of the imperfect in direct discourse. The principal distinction between the two types of criticism is that Chevalier and Débax look, in their works, for a more precise method of qualifying the effects of linguistic manipulation. Perhaps the most significant aspect of their work is the fact that they bear constantly in mind that *Romancero* results from a conjunction between the prevailing conditions of transmission and the material each *romance* seeks to present. Moreover, the *architecture temporelle* critics consider the *Romancero* to be a product of ordinary language and its common usages. This point of view is not shared, as will be seen in the following section, by all *Romancero* critics.

F. "Romancero"

Of the numerous theories to arise from the discussion of *Romancero* grammar, perhaps the most radical is the approach taken by Stephen Gilman in his article "On 'Romancero' as a Poetic Language."[24] Gilman's claim here is that the language of the ballads results from a "verbal situation" that bears no resemblance either to ordinary speech or to its "literary" counterpart. Rather, the remarkable characteristics of *Romancero* grammar discussed above constitute a separate and unrelated language—a notion which Gilman reinforces through distinctive punctuation; "Romancero," written between quotation marks, refers to the language, not the corpus.

Gilman's theory of "Romancerò" as a poetic language stems from his previous work on tense in the *Poema del Cid*[25] and from a study of Szertics's *Tiempo y verbo en el Romancero Viejo,*[26] which he reviewed. In the latter piece, Gilman concludes that:

> not only does the *Romancero* exhibit the scope of a language, but also its characteristic syntax is so radically different from that of normal speech usage as to go beneath the level of deviation which can be explained stylistically. (340)

In the former piece, Gilman determines that the linguistic system of the *Poema*–found to be a stylistic phenomenon of that work–bears little relation to the ballad speech of the *romances*. The irregular use of tenses in the *Poema del Cid*, where the "professional 'juglar' . . . worshipped but never impersonated" (157) the hero's speech, is unlike the loss of temporal reference Gilman finds characteristic of "Romancero," where "singer and listener become one and the same" (157). In fact, Gilman remarks, "the earliest 'romances' are far closer grammatically to those collected today than they are to the *Poema del Cid*" (rev. 339).

"Romancero," according to Gilman, is an atemporal language. The verb morphemes that in Spanish grammar are associated with temporal sequence lose all reference to *consecutio temporum* (a term favored by Gilman in his work on the *PMC*) in "Romancero." As Gilman describes this phenomenon:

> In "Romancero" tenses lose temporal reference, they are no longer chained to a single point of view, and their coexistence expresses not a mixture of times, but an abandonment of time, itself. They are a means of directing us inwards, into a language not our own, a language which transforms fantasy into reality. ("On 'Romancero'" 159)

The principal advantage to differentiating ballad speech from ordinary speech seems to be that a "Romancero" critic, unlike the critics discussed in previous sections of this chapter, has no need to reconcile any of the data of Spanish grammar with the facts of the language of the *Romancero*. The very nature of "Romancero" obviates the necessity of seeking grammatical explanations for such unusual features as the mixture of verb morphemes in the ballads. These linguistic anomalies are instead explained by the unique verbal situation created in "Romancero," where "the frontier between the 'now' and the 'then,' the here and the beyond, the 'literary character' and the perceiving awareness" collapses ("On 'Romancero'" 157). The example of Spitzer's difficulty with the intrusion of the imperfect into the dialogue portions of the *Romance de Abenámar* is, Gilman feels, symptomatic of the approach which ignores this unique verbal situation. Other stylistic approaches, in their recourse to the standard works of reference on Spanish syntax, similarly neglect the complete loss of temporal reference basic to the theory of "Romancero." Thus, many of the perplexities concerning ballad speech are heightened rather than avoided in the stylistic approach.

Gilman's theory of "Romancero" as a poetic language has the further attraction of providing an explanation for the "absolute unity of form"[27] which distinguishes the *Romancero* from other European ballad traditions. The thesis that the ballads were composed in "Romancero" rather than, say, Castilian, would account for what Menéndez Pidal has termed, "lo inimitable," or the singular characteristics of the *Romancero* which can never be successfully duplicated by a written composition. Furthermore, the notion of "Romancero" as a unique verbal situation in which several voices merge to participate in the ballad performance assigns an explanation to the often-remarked impression of immediacy given by the *romances*.[28] In the erasure of the boundary between the present singer and a past speaker, which Gilman claims is effected, or "linguistically invoked," by "Romancero," the listener is made to feel a party to the circumstances proposed by the ballad. Moreover, the singer, who does not imitate a style, but rather, who speaks "a language which he knows quite as well as the prosaic variety used for daily communication" (rev. 340-41), addresses a listener, to whom "Romancero" is "perfectly and intuitively familiar" (rev. 340). This would account for the curious bond between the singer and the audience that has been observed by modern students of oral literature.

However appealing the theory of "Romancero" as a poetic language might seem in its avoidance of the problems that have consistently plagued ballad critics, there are several drawbacks to considering ballad speech as separate from the language used in daily communication. First of all, there is a good deal of evidence of a correspondence between the language of the ballads and the spoken language which dominates at each stage of ballad production. Lapesa, in his chapter on the language of the *cantares de gesta* and the *Romancero viejo,* points out that a discussion of the linguistic details of the two genres would constitute an entire history of the evolution of the Spanish language:

> En el siglo XII el castellano era un dialecto románico recién constituido, pujante, pero inseguro, carente de la fijeza que sólo un prolongado cultivo literario llega a proporcionar. Hacia 1550, cuando se imprimen en Amberes los *Cancioneros de Romances* y en Zaragoza la *Silva de Romances,* el castellano, ya lengua española, había llegado a su madurez. (9)

Lapesa's examples of grammatical forms which conform to popular usage contemporaneous with epic and ballad production include some of the very forms that Gilman claims establish the basis of "Romancero" as a poetic language. During the Middle Ages, Lapesa says, the distribution of functions between the different tenses was far less clear than it is today:

> *Canté* podía ser pretérito absoluto, esto es, indefinido, o perfecto; por eso no hay distinción formal en *Mío Cid* entre "Vos agora *llegastes*" y "nos *viniemos* anoch." El tiempo *cantara, dixiera* conservaba el significado de pluscuamperfecto de indicativo, esto es, el etimológico heredado de *amaveram, dixeram*. . . . Pero con gran frecuencia, sobre todo en el Romancero, se emplea como simple pasado, conforme ocurre en gallego y portugués. (20-21)

The "liberties" of verbal tense usage described above manifest themselves equally, according to Lapesa, in the example of the imperfect that appears in the dialogue portion of *Abenámar.* Lapesa, using the stylistic argument, claims that the substitution of the imperfect for the present tense results from "evidente sentido artístico del lenguaje" (22). However, he argues, this "artistic sense" depends on general linguistic knowledge (20-21). This is different from Gilman's conception of a singer "speaking a ballad-specific language."

Lapesa's chapter on the language of the *cantares de gesta* and the *Romancero viejo* predates both of the articles in which Gilman calls for the establishment of "Romancero" as a poetic language. Yet Lapesa anticipates, in his concluding remarks of the chapter, this very argument. He writes:

> Pero ni siquiera de los romances carolingios puede decirse que empleen una lengua especial. En la literatura española el lenguaje épico no constituye dialecto indepen- diente. Tampoco es una forma de expresión petrificada: en cada momento de la producción épica responde esencialmente al estado lingüístico que dominaba en el habla común. (28)

Lapesa's discussion of the ways in which language and the epic and ballad literature show parallel development functions as a paleographic counter- example to Gilman's argument. Lapesa deals primarily with written examples, imposing an historico-linguistic point of view on his data. Other evidence that calls Gilman's theory into question comes from *Romancero* scholars who have studied the modern oral tradition. Although Gilman does speak, in "On 'Romancero' as a Poetic Language," of other ballad traditions as well as the *Romancero,* indicating that they share similar linguistic effects (156), his notion of the role of the singer *vis-à-vis* the grammatical properties of the Spanish ballad runs counter to the investigations of, for example, Armistead and Silverman. Armistead and Silverman's studies point to cultural circum- stances as the agent responsible for conditioning the composition of a *romance.* As they remark in their article, "A Judeo-Spanish *Kompla* and Its Greek Counterpart":[29]

> We have uncovered a number of narrative poems in *romance* meter which have no counterparts elsewhere in Hispanic tradition, but which derive, rather, from the balladry of the Balkan peoples among whom the Spanish Jews have lived for almost 500 years—notably from the rich balladic tradition of Greece. (262)

The implication of this observation is that the *Romancero,* as a poetic tradition, is far more flexible than a poetic language such as Gilman's "Romancero." It allows into it material that neither results from artistic manipulation nor from the joint tenancy of speaker and listener in the *romance* that Gilman calls the "verbal situation" of "Romancero." Rather, the studies of Armistead and Silverman, which look closely at the communities which transmit the ballads rather than some implied "speaker" and "listener," evince the *Romancero* as more a vehicle for the manifestation of a cultural situation than for the "poetically and linguistically induced communion" spoken of by Gilman ("On 'Romancero' " 156).

The account by Rina Benmayor of "A Greek *Tragoúdi* in the Repertoire of a Judeo-Spanish Ballad Singer" further establishes the tie between the content of a ballad and the circumstances which surround its singers. Benmayor's discussion of the influence of the cultural and linguistic context of the Judeo-Spanish corpus focuses on the "human dimension" in the ballad art. She points out that "an art form such as oral ballads is not self-generative. . . . it is people who transmit the *Romancero*."[30] This is quite a different argument from Gilman's, which seems to divest the singer of an active participation in the linguistic creation of the ballad, instead directing attention away from Benmayor's "human dimension." The metaphysical communion which Gilman claims is afforded by "Romancero" lends to *language,* not people, the active function in ballad art. In "Romancero," there is only passive shareholding by singer—and audience as well. As Gilman comments, "we . . . are called upon, transfixed, compelled to participate by the abrupt thrust of the vocative in our interior silence" ("On 'Romancero' " 156).

There is no doubt that the language of the *Romancero* is, in many ways, idiosyncratic. However, the studies cited in this section, as well as in later ones, suggest that the "Romancero"-as-a-poetic-language solution is equally as problematic as the more traditional approaches.

G. The Performance Factor

The various approaches to the remarkable features of *Romancero* grammar outlined in this chapter share a common goal: each seeks to explain the characteristic patterning of tense and aspect in the *Romancero* through a study of the information contained in the vast collection of *romances* that exists today. Consequently, as explanations of the *Romancero* grammar, the above approaches all participate in at least one major shortcoming; this is that they fail to adequately consider the circumstances that surround *Romancero* production. It is true that all of the critics, with the exception of those that concern themselves exclusively with rhyme scheme, metrics, and other purely structural factors, speak of a "narrator" and an "audience" when discussing the *Romancero.* Only Gilman, however, explicitly recognizes that the situation which obtains between these two groups is a verbal one, but he mistakenly—as will be later demonstrated—believes that the circumstances which surround *Romancero* production bear no relation to the ordinary speech situation of daily discourse.

The *Romancero* is orally narrated literature; its production relies heavily on the conditions which prevail at the time of each *romance*'s performance.

The special properties of the *Romancero* that have been discussed thus far result from the fact that it is, as Menéndez Pidal has commented:

> una poesía dinámica, capaz de suscitar múltiples desenvolvimientos en la imaginación del que la repite. No es obra conclusa, definitivamente corregida y acabada sobre el papel por el arte personal de un escritor; no tiene esa inmovilidad estatuaria; es, por el contrario, un ser animado, que perdura, no en la fijeza de la escritura y del libro, sino en el mudable canto del pueblo. (1: 42)

To disregard, as the stylistic critics, assonance-argument critics, and Gilman do, the assumptions and attitudes that the narrators of the *romances* have towards their audience, and vice versa, is to omit from examination an essential feature of any verbal situation. The singers and their public are the essence of *Romancero* production. They are the determining factors with respect to both the language and the content of a *Romancero* text.

In *Romancero* composition and transmission there is a constant interaction between the singer and the physically present audience, and although the audience may be somewhat restricted in its communicative role (expressions of approval, disapproval, body language, etc.), it nevertheless exercises an immediate and ongoing control over the structure and content of the text. The singer of a *romance,* who receives continuous feedback from the listeners and who, to begin with, may be familiar with the audience's beliefs and attitudes, as well as what will please them,[31] manipulates the form of the text to accomodate the demeanor of the group to whom it is performed. Like the singing of a national anthem before an athletic contest, the performance of a *romance* signals a kind of collusion between the participants in the oral literary situation, and the voice of the singer cooperates with that of the listeners.

Menéndez Pidal has described the interaction between singer and audience during *Romancero* production as a "collaboration," tacitly suggesting that the language of the *romances* implies a particular oral literary situation. He comments:

> Todo el que disfruta una obra de arte le añade algo de su propia sensibilidad, colaborando con el artista. . . . la colaboración del que la disfruta se hace más expresa y activa en las fugaces variantes que se introducen en la obra misma. (1: 42-43)

As Menéndez Pidal suggests, it is in the numerous variants of the *romances* that the collaborative phenomenon of *Romancero* production and reproduction is most strikingly manifested. Examples from the *Romancero* that illustrate this phenomenon as well as its effect on the language of the variants of a text are easily found.

The *Romance de Tarquino y Lucrecia* is a text whose many versions indicate the importance of the attitudes and aspirations of the audience for whom it is performed in the linguistic structuring of the work. The story in the *romance,* reminiscent of Livy's account in the *Roman History* of the fall of the Tarquini line in the sixth century B.C. through the dishonoring of Lucretia, a Roman matron,[32] tells of the confrontation between a chaste woman and a powerful member of a ruling family. However, as the following Judeo-Spanish version of the story indicates, in the *Romancero,* the cultural postures and historical circumstances of the groups that propagate the Roman legend have led to significant changes in the story's structure and content:

Romance de Tarquino y Lucrecia

	a	b
1	O qué rey de las romansas	que Tarquinos se llamava.
2		por la su puerta pasava.
3	La reina que lo vido	
4	—¿Qué buxcax, mi rey Tarquinos,	talas horas por mi sala?
5	—Vuestros amores, mi dama,	no me dexan reposar.
6	Y si tal me los atorgas	seyas reina encoronada.
7	Y si tal no me las atorgas	con me spada seyas matada.
8	—Más prefiero morir con honra	y no vivir desfamada.
9	Que no digan la mi gente,	—De un cristió fue namoroza.
10	Estas palavras diziendo,	el cuchillo l'enfincó.
11	Y la romansa se acavó.[33]	

The *Romance de Tarquino y Lucrecia* cited above belongs to the eastern Judeo-Spanish tradition. It was recorded by Benmayor during fieldwork in 1973 in Seattle, Washington. Clearly, this *romance* was intended for a Sephardic audience which would recognize and appreciate the cultural taboo represented in terms of the struggle between Christians and Jews—with modern implications of an interdiction against intermarriage. Using the language of this Judeo-Christian conflict (e.g., the "dishonor" of relations with a "Christian" [8 and 9b]), the singer appeals to her audience to discover Lucrecia's great virtue in the fact that a *Jewish* woman (not Roman, as in Livy's version and other *Romancero* texts) chose death when faced with seduction by a Christian man.[34]

The language of the above version of the *Romance de Tarquino y Lucrecia* demonstrates the collaboration between singer and audience during the performance[35] through its play on marked lexical items such as *cristió* (10b) and *gente* (9a)—here used to denote Lucrecia's peer group. The singer chooses these items to establish a bond with an audience which might be somewhat less interested in a text which seems otherwise to detail the events of an historically, geographically, and culturally remote situation. In other words, the language of the text responds to the societal values or postulates of its audience, bringing new meaning to the ancient legend.

Another example from the *Romancero* indicates specifically the effect that the interaction between singers and listeners during the production of a *romance* has on the grammar of a text. This example, from the archaic tradition, has been documented by D. W. Foster in an interesting article on the *Romance de Alora la bien cercada*.[36] Foster writes of the situation in which singers who perform for Christian audiences wish to direct attention to the Moorish "side of the story." In telling Christians about the siege of Alora, in which Moorish treachery against the Christian army reached a peak, the singer of the *romance*, who knew that the attitude of the audience towards the Moors was hostile, was constrained to find what Foster terms "a structural resolution of the problem of rhetorically engaging audience sympathy" (392). The singer accomplished this end in the ballad through language, using an eight-line apostrophe to Alora at the outset of the *romance*, followed by an adynation ("Viérades") in the ninth line, and an ingenious manipulation of the Spanish word for *Moor* throughout the remainder of the text (394).

When one considers the type of language used in *Romancero* composition and transmission to be a consequence of the oral literary situation of a performance, the problem of accounting for the characteristic syntax and lexis of the *romances* takes on new dimensions. Stylistic criticism, discussed earlier in this chapter, implies a much more passive audience for the *romances* than actual examples of *Romancero* performance suggest. The stylistic critics view singers as manipulators of language for the purposes of exercising control over the imagination, attention, and attention span of their listeners. The audience, according to this view, *reacts* to the singer's craft, and has control only over the decision of whether to hear the singer out, or to leave, cutting short the performance. In actuality, as an example from Parry and Lord's experience illustrates, the audience does regulate the lengthening and shortening of a composition in accordance with the "feedback" it provides to the singer:

> The singer begins to tell his tale. If he is fortunate, he may find it possible to sing until he is tired without interruption from the audience. After a rest he will continue, if his audience still wishes. This may last until he finishes the song, and if his listeners are propitious and his mood heightened by their interest, he may lengthen his tale, savoring each descriptive passage. It is more likely that, instead of having this ideal occasion the singer will realize shortly after beginning that his audience is not receptive, and hence he will shorten his song so that it may be finished within the limit of time for which he feels the audience may be counted on. Or, if he misjudges, he may simply never finish the song. Leaving out of consideration for the moment the question of the talent of the singer, one can say that the length of the song depends upon the audience. One of the reasons also why different singings of the same song by the same man vary most in their endings is that the end of a song is sung less often by the singer.[37]

However, as was seen in the *Romance de Tarquino y Lucrecia* and in the *Romance de Alora la bien cercada,* the audience also may exercise a *substantive* control over a text. It is not, of course, always easy to quantify the precise nature through which this control is effected, and perhaps this is a reason for the avoidance of the "performance factor" in *Romancero* language by so many critics. Yet examples from both the modern and the archaic traditions give indications that singers and their audiences do communicate during performance.

Given the oral literary situations described above, in which singers direct their compositions to an audience which in turn influences their actualization and creation, it becomes apparent that the stylistic approach to *Romancero* grammar, though important, is not sufficient as an explanation for the characteristic syntax and lexis of the *romances.* The approach suggested by the proponents of *architecture temporelle* in *Romancero* grammar relates somewhat more convincingly to the concept of collaboration between singer and audience during oral performance. *Architecture temporelle* suggests a kind of manipulation by narrators of verbal tense and aspect which involves a direct interaction, or discourse, of verbal forms as they position the audience both within and outside the events described in the narrative. The audience is thus integrated into the text through linguistic maneuvers. However, like the other critical approaches discussed in this chapter, the audience is assigned by *architecture temporelle* a passive role in *Romancero* production, and no consideration is given to the part played in the *romance* by audience attitudes and beliefs as they are reflected in the grammar of the compositions.

In order to successfully explain the distinctive syntax and lexis discussed at the beginning of this chapter, it is necessary to take into account such extralinguistic data as the participation of listeners in the oral literary situation. The circumstances that exist during the performance of a *romance* may be, in an important way, responsible for the manner in which the texts are constructed.

The grammar of the *Romancero* implies an oral literary situation. Accordingly, it is essential for critics to concern themselves with the context of *Romancero* production and reproduction—i.e., the historical, political, and cultural parameters of a *romance*—in order to gain an understanding of the characteristic language used in its composition. Sociolinguistics is an approach that considers the most valuable statements about linguistic behavior to be those that take into account the entire social context of a verbal situation. Within a sociolinguistic approach to the *Romancero,* the attitudes and information that an audience brings to the performance of a *romance* take on paramount importance. They are considered in terms of the effect they have on the language of the compositions. The following chapters of this study will discuss the application of a sociolinguistic approach to the problem of *Romancero* grammar.

3

A Sociolinguistic Approach
to Narrative Structure in the *Romancero*

A. Introduction

Sociolinguistics takes a contextual approach to narrative, relating the grammatical complexities found in literary texts and oral relations to the circumstances surrounding their production. This type of approach, which differs radically from that of most of the critics discussed in the previous chapter of this study, links the values, or basic postulates, of different societies to the differing decisions singers or writers take in the grammatical structuring of their compositions. It considers the remarkable features of the *Romancero* grammar to be *evaluative* devices, or media through which events in the narrative can be interpreted and reformulated during the production and reproduction of the *Romancero*.

The point of a sociolinguistic approach is to call attention to the characteristic patterning of narratives and to connect this patterning with the type of communicative activity which takes place during the (oral) literary situation. William Labov, a sociolinguist who has focused on the syntactic properties of oral narratives and the social contexts within which they are produced, has discussed in particular this issue of communication between narrator and audience during performance. Although Labov's research is inclined specifically towards the study of unrehearsed oral versions of personal experience,[1] his insistence that narrative language be recognized as a result of a conscious selection by a narrator of grammatical structures already present in ordinary speech marks his approach as a methodology quite generally useful and important to the entire field of narratology, including *Romancero* studies. Labov's investigations, which are designed to determine the characteristic patternings of personal anecdotes and their connection to the communicative activity that takes place during the course of narration, bear directly on the type of critical endeavor prescribed for the *Romancero* in the previous chapter.

25

Labov, in a paper entitled "The Transformation of Experience in Narrative Syntax,"[2] suggests a framework for the analysis of syntactic and lexical complexities. This framework provides a precise method for cataloguing the grammatical structures found in particular narratives. It also allows for an effective correlation to be made between language and context. The value of this framework for *Romancero* criticism is that, at the same time that it provides a way of carefully studying the language which is found in' the *Romancero*, it permits an explicit relation to be made between the *romances* and their social and historical context.

The aim of the present chapter is to discuss the advantages of the type of sociolinguistic approach outlined above to the study of *Romancero* grammar. This chapter will also consider the application to the *romances* of the framework for oral narrative proposed in William Labov's sociolinguistic investigations.

B. Narrative Structure

Narrative is, in general, a recapitulation of events through a verbal sequence of clauses which matches the sequence of events described. In its most fundamental sense, a narrative consists of a series of temporally ordered, or narrative, clauses, whose syntax follows the basic pattern detailed in section 2A of this study—i.e., a series of eight elements, without hierarchical phrase structure, constituting the sentence adverbial, the subject-noun phrase, and the verb phrase.

The excerpt from a news article found in table 1 may be seen as an example of this basic syntax. Its fundamental simplicity calls attention to the more complex elements that sometimes do occur in other types of narrative.[3]

Some narratives consist exclusively of the type of clauses displayed in this excerpt. Other, more fully developed, narratives may contain a variety of elements of narrative structure. William Labov's analyses of oral narratives of personal experience suggest that these elements may be divided into six sections: the Abstract, the Orientation, the Complicating Action, the Evaluation, the Resolution, and the Coda. These six sections structure the narrative as answers to the following questions:

1. What was this about? (Abstract)
2. Who, when, what, where? (Orientation)
3. Then what happened? (Complicating Action)
4. So what? (Evaluation)
5. What finally happened? (Resolution)
6. Where did it all end up? (Coda)[4]

TABLE 1

Basic Narrative Syntax in an Unevaluated Narrative

1[a]	2	3	4	5	6	7	8
	el hombre		roció	su cuerpo	con cuatro botellas de gasolina		
			se encadenó	a una bomba de agua		en la principal plaza de Cracovia	
							a eso de las 8 de la mañana

Source for narrative: *El Diario-La Prensa* [New York], 23 Mar. 1979: 5, col. 1.

[a] Numbers refer to the components of basic narrative syntax described on p. 8 of this study.

Labov's paradigm for the structure of a fully formed narrative applies specifically to the personal anecdotes he collected during fieldwork in various neighborhoods of the eastern United States. The following story is one such example:

> (What was the most important fight that
>   you remember, one that sticks in your
>   mind . . .)
> Well, one (I think) was with a girl.
> Like I was a kid, you know,
> And she was the baddest girl, the
>   *baddest girl in the neighborhood.*
> If you didn't bring her candy to school,
>   she would punch you in the mouth;
> And you had to kiss her
>   when she'd tell you.
> This girl was only about 12 years old, man,
> but she was a killer.
> She didn't take no junk;
> She whupped all her brothers.
> And I came to school one day
> and I didn't have no money.
> My ma wouldn't give me no money.
> And I played hookies one day.
> (She) put something on me.
> I played hookies, man,
> so I said, you know, I'm not gonna play
>   hookies no more
>   'cause I don't wanna get a whupping.
> So I go to school
> and this girl says, "Where's the candy?"
> I said, "I don't have it."
> She says, powww!
> So I says to myself, "There's gonna be times my
> mother won't give me money
> because we're a poor family
> And I can't take this all, you know, every time
>   she don't give me any money."
> So I say, "Well, I just gotta fight this girl.
> She gonna hafta whup me."
> And I hit the girl: powwww!
> and I put something on it.
> I win the fight.
> That was one of the most important. (358-59)

There is much evidence to suggest, however, that the paradigm Labov uses is equally applicable to a wide variety of narratives, including those found in literature. These narratives share with Labov's anecdotes "similar ways of displaying and contemplating experience" but may differ in their methods of composition and transmission.[5]

The *Romancero* is oral literature. It is narrative composed under certain literary constraints—e.g., rhyme scheme, meter—but it is transmitted to a live audience by singers. As oral performance, the *Romancero* shares with Labov's narratives some of the same formal and functional features. For example, both may be orally composed and both types of narrative may be refined and corrected through repeated performance (although Labov does not address this issue in his study). It is not surprising to find, therefore, that both the oral narrative of personal experience and the *Romancero* use similar structures in their compositions. These structures are characteristic of the face-to-face confrontation with a live audience that is implicit in all oral narrative.

In applying Labov's paradigm to the *Romancero*, it is necessary, as will later be pointed out, to make certain modifications. In general, however, the paradigm speaks directly to many of the most troublesome issues in *Romancero* analysis.

C. Evaluation

The most interesting and consequential element of Labov's paradigm for the analysis of narrative structures with respect to the critical issues concerning *Romancero* grammar is the Evaluation. The Evaluation refers to the section of a narrative in which there is the greatest concentration of linguistic complexities.[6] These complexities, which are frequently "relatively minor syntactic element[s] in the narrative clause" (Labov 378), express the *tellability* of a narrative—i.e., why the events of the narrative are felt to be reportable within a particular oral literary situation. They also function to interpret for the audience the attitude towards the events of the narrative they, as listeners, are expected to adopt.

There are a number of different ways in which evaluation in the narrative may be effected. For example, if a narrator interrupts a story to insert a comment such as *¡Qué decepción!* or *¡tanta era la afrenta!* the evaluation is known as *external evaluation.* On the other hand, if an idea or a feeling is quoted as having occurred to the narrator at a certain point in the narrative, and there is no interruption of the course of the story to address the audience, the evaluation is said to be *internal* to the narrative, or *embedded* in it. Finally, and perhaps most interesting, are those evaluative devices that are internal to the narrative's very sentences. Labov, in his investigations, points to four major headings under which these evaluative elements may be classified. They are the intensifiers, the comparators, the correlatives, and the explicatives

(378). These headings are described below, with appropriate examples from Spanish grammar:

1. Intensifiers: an intensifier singles out a particular event in the narrative and strengthens it by means of gestures, expressive phonology (e.g., lengthened vowels), quantifiers (e.g., the use of *todos* in the sentence "Tienen todos carteles de mago"), repetition, or ritual utterance (e.g., "Que Alá te guarde").

2. Comparators: comparators introduce a syntactic complexity into the narrative in that they compare events that actually occurred with those that were never actualized. They include negatives, futures, modals, questions, imperatives, or-clauses, superlatives, and comparatives (e.g., *como*).

3. Correlatives: a correlative joins together different events realized in the narrative. Examples are appended participles, where one or more gerunds are aligned with the tense marker and the verb *estar* deleted, double (triple, etc.) attributives (e.g., *la agencia noticiosa oficial polaca PAP*), and appositives (e.g., *tierras, rojas, islas*).

4. Explicatives: explicatives consist of explicit evaluative clauses such as conjunctions (e.g., *mientras, sin embargo*), or causals (e.g., *por, porque*) that enter into the narrative for the purpose of explicating or evaluating a particular action.

The excerpt cited in section 3B of this study as an example of basic narrative syntax is an illustration of relatively unevaluated narrative. Although it concerns an ultimately reportable matter—i.e., the public self-immolation of a political dissident—the reporter of the story makes no particular attempt in his description to insist upon the tragic, uncommon, or unusual aspects of the event. He uses simple preterite tenses and complements; a simple subject; and manner, locative, and temporal clauses that, although somewhat richer than the subject and verb phrases, do not match the complexity of the evaluative devices described, for example, in Labov's schema.

Unlike the news report, the exemplary *Romance de la morilla burlada* discussed in section 2A of this study involves a series of verbal maneuvers that easily fit the sociolinguist's specifications for a fully evaluated narrative. These verbal maneuvers, referred to in chapter 2 as "remarkable" characteristics of the *Romancero* grammar, are in fact evaluative devices; they call attention to the *raison d'être* of the *romance* through a departure from basic narrative syntax. In this manner, the imperative, negative, and interrogative clauses of the *romance* may be considered as comparators, introducing a syntactic complexity into the narrative that calls attention to nonactualized situations. The imperfect and present tense clauses may be seen as correlatives, joining together different events in the *romance* in order to suspend the story's action and highlight particular situations. The dialogue may be seen as an explicative, transferring the listeners' attention back in time in order to "explain" the third person narrative. Other syntactic complexities, found throughout the *romance,* have similar effects, illustrating Labov's premise that departures from the basic narrative syntax have a marked evaluative force (378).

The application of a sociolinguistic approach to the analysis of language in the *Romance de la morilla burlada* results in a reappraisal of the text that is worth noting. According to the paradigm proposed by Labov for the structure of a fully formed narrative, the *Romance de la morilla burlada* may be divided into the following sections: [7]

> Orientation: 1a-2a
> Abstract: 2b
> Complicating Action: 3a-3b
> Evaluation: 4a-8b
> Coda: 9a-11b

The Evaluation section of the *romance* coincides with the portion of the work composed solely of dialogue. In it, the narrator departs from the basic narrative syntax used in the simple recounting of the story in order to register the authoritative voice of the *morilla,* who is the speaking *persona* in the *romance.* It is the attitudes and beliefs of Moraima that guide the audience in the ballad. However, the special evaluative properties of dialogue allow this guidance to create a kind of evaluative irony in the *romance.* The dialogue between the Moorish woman and the nonauthoritative (since he is not the speaking *persona* of the *romance*) Christian unexpectedly shows the listeners precisely those attitudes they are *not* to adopt. They ought not to adopt the attitudes and beliefs of Moraima, who continually refers to herself as *cuitada.* She, although a victim, is dangerous; she spontaneously collaborates to protect a man who she thinks is a Moorish murderer. Furthermore, the special properties of dialogue show the audience that the evaluative comments of the Christian impostor mean something other than what they say. The seeming duplicity of the Christian is really a demonstration of his artful cunning. The dialogue portrays him as clever enough to successfully appropriate both the language and the culture of the Moors, thus outsmarting them. Though a liar and a *burlador,* he is, in effect, a victor in his villainy, for the dynamic which makes this story tellable in the Christian context is the statement, made through the syntax and lexis of the ballad, that the Moors, though clever, were outrivaled by the even cleverer Christians who, as a result, triumphed over them. The

Christian, who is made by the singer to speak in commands and threats, succeeds not only in deceiving the Moorish Moraima but also in intimidating and
subduing her. In this way the narrator appeals syntactically to the Christian
interlocutors' sense of superiority over the infidel.

D. Limitations of Labovian Analysis with Respect to the *Romancero*

The *Romancero* is a collective creation, anonymously composed and orally
transmitted within the popular domain. *Romances* are infinitely alterable
by their singers and, although they generally retain some "flavor" of the
events they commemorate, they are characteristically open to continuous
renovation and re-creation within different historical and social contexts.

The oral narratives elicited and analyzed by William Labov are, unlike the
romances, unrehearsed narratives of personal experience. Although potentially
open to re-creation under different sets of circumstances, these narratives are
never specifically designed for retelling. They are, rather, spontaneously
composed anecdotes told by nonprofessional (although in many cases talented)
narrators, for the purposes of answering a question specially intended to
elicit a casual rendering of past experience.[8]

The differences in composition and transmission between the *Romancero*
and the oral narrative of personal experience may account for some of the
different preferences for evaluative technique found in the two types of
narratives. For example, many *romances,* which were composed by professional *juglares* in medieval Spain, exhibit a predilection for dialogue, while
this device seems somewhat rarer in conversational narrative—although Labov
does include several examples of dialogue in his study (356-59). The *juglares*
may have preferred dialogue because it allowed them to display their dramatic
skills (imitating various voices, gestures, etc.) during performance. It also
enabled them to effect certain political responses in their audience, an object
not indicated for Labov's narratives, but essential to some Spanish oral literature. As Julio Rodríguez-Puértolas has pointed out,[9] such structures in the
narrative function in oral poetry (here he addresses himself to the epic in
particular) to "actualize" past historical events in order to rally audience
support for contemporary policies:

> Parece evidente que un poema épico, si bien relata sucesos ocurridos en el pasado,
> los maneja de tal modo que los actualiza intencionalmente, y los trae al presente
> con objeto de incitar y animar a los oyentes a imitar las viejas heroicidades. (25)

Dialogue is also particularly apt as an evaluative device in the *Romancero*
because it structures free clauses (i.e., clauses having no temporal juncture

between them) in such a way as to both further the action of the *romance* and evaluate the events described. This is to say that the singer may use dialogue in a *romance* to expand upon particular events in dramatic form, while permitting a protagonist of the story to guide the audience through the situations developed. The "guidance" afforded through the dialogue is apparent in its participants' use of certain grammatical items. These items, which appear in Labov's framework as complexities, are marked within the dialogue structure of the *romances* as indicators of the relationship between the speakers. For example, when the Christian impostor cries, " ¡Si Alá te guarde de mal!" in the *Romance de la morilla burlada,* he is using a ritual utterance which he knows will be recognized by the Moorish woman as evidence of his kinship with her. Furthermore, only a fellow Moor would use the lexical items he does, which are clearly of Arabic origin. His deception is of the most devious sort, but as the singer shows through the use of direct discourse, the Moorish woman is convinced of his authenticity and is caused by his words to be sympathetic towards his plea. By leaving the conversation between the Christian and Moraima in the direct discourse mode, the singer of the *Romance de la morilla burlada* most effectively points out to the listeners the cunning manner in which the Moorish woman was deceived.

Furthermore, in the *Romancero,* singers may use the property of conversational exchange which often identifies the patterns of orientation of the participants as a kind of "power struggle" to demonstrate to the audience the competition for domination between the protagonists of a *romance.* The dialogue in the Moraima ballad is again representative: by the commands (*Ábraseme*), threats ("si no me abres tú, mi vida,   aquí me verás matar" [8]), and deceptive language (Arabic) mentioned earlier, the Christian overpowers Moraima and gains his wishes. No physical exertion is necessary, for as the singer shows, the Christian's words are his weapons.

Dialogue also evaluates the perspective of an audience within the oral literary situation of the *Romancero.* In many instances, when audience familiarity with the events dealt with in a *romance* is presupposed, dialogue may be used by a singer to single out a particular situation and dramatize it, rather than risk losing audience attention through the superfluous rehearsal of a well-known story. This perhaps accounts for some of the fragmentation found in *romances* where the only passage preserved is the dialogue.[10]

Evaluative devices in the *Romancero* such as dialogue represent departures from basic narrative syntax that do not involve individual narrative clauses but rather are large scale evaluative structures.[11] These broad, technical devices do not fall within the scope of Labov's analysis of the oral narrative of personal experience, which is limited to syntactic complexities in discrete narrative units. A theory which considers evaluation in the *romances,* however, must accommodate large-scale structures such as dialogue, for they are heavily relied upon in the *Romancero* for evaluative purposes. Furthermore, these devices are intrinsic to the narrative structure of the *romances* and they play an important part in the characteristic grammatical patternings of the *Romancero*.[1 2]

For the purposes of analyzing the role of evaluation in the *Romancero* grammar, both the syntactically complex clauses (of which dialogue is often composed) and dialogue itself must be considered. In this manner, some of the anomalies of the *Romancero* grammar that result from Labov's clause-based framework (e.g., present tense usage in direct discourse) may be seen as regularities within the broader evaluative structure of dialogue.

A second non-clause-based evaluative category that seems to take on increased importance in the *Romancero* is that of the *marked lexical item*. Marked lexical items are words that function throughout the course of a narrative to establish and maintain a kind of rapport between narrators and audience within a particular oral literary situation. For example, in the previously mentioned Judeo-Spanish *Romance de Tarquino y Lucrecia,* a term such as *cristió* is marked with respect to the circumstances within which the *romance* was performed. The introduction of this word into the text brings a conspiratorial togetherness to the Sephardic oral literary situation where singer and audience share common concerns for group survival. It is essential to the point of this *romance* that Tarquino be identified as a Christian—a common enemy of the group. As will later be shown, the term *judío* is similarly marked within some Christian singer-audience contexts.

Another function of the marked lexical item within the narrative clauses of a *romance* is specific to the dialogue portion of the text. One of the systems by which participants in a dialogue identify themselves or react to others is lexicoreferential. Certain lexical items in the *romances* (e.g., the Arabic terms used in the *Romance de la morilla burlada,* and the *morilla engañada* who repeatedly calls herself *cuitada*) may be marked with respect to the effects they potentially have on fellow participants in the discourse. Moreover, these lexical items may assist in evaluating for the audience the type of guidance they can expect to receive from the protagonists. As was earlier mentioned, the audience, through the use of the word *cuitada* in Moraima's self-identification, is discouraged from adopting the attitudes and beliefs of the Moorish woman.

Semantic characteristics, such as those seen through the lexis of the above exemplary *romances,* introduce significant complexities into the narrative clauses of the *Romancero*. They do not, however, function specifically within the syntactic structuring of the clauses, but may simply act as "beacons" to the audience during the course of a performance. Because they do play an evaluative role within the oral literary situation, marked lexical items must also be accounted for in an analysis of *Romancero* grammar.

The nature of the speech situation in which a linguistic action occurs—whether its participants be speakers and listeners or singers and audiences—is what determines the verbal structure of a narrative. The troubles that critics have traditionally had with the structure and contents of *romances* in which a Christian *juglar* sings the praises of the Moors, or shows a Christian's cruelty towards them (e.g., suggestions that these *romances* can only be explained by postulating Arabic, and not Christian, origin) are alleviated through sociolinguistic analysis, which is dependent upon the context of the speech acts recorded.[13] The sociolinguistic perspective takes into account the full circumstances of the performance of a *romance* and renders its syntax and lexis meaningful through a discussion of the broader questions of what the singer is trying to do in forming his or her *romance* and how the audience reacts upon hearing it.

The following chapter of this study will apply the framework for narrative analysis discussed here—including the modifications suggested in terms of *Romancero* grammar—to a group of *romances* that incorporate in their narrative structure both large-scale evaluators and syntactically complex clauses. These *romances* form part of the *Romancero del rey don Pedro*, a ballad cycle which responds in an interesting way to the poetic and ideological context of the late Middle Ages. The kind of study that was suggested in this chapter for the *Romance de la morilla burlada* will be expanded in the next into a full-fledged proposal for an analysis of *Romancero* grammar based on a sociolinguistic approach to the narrative.

4

A Sociolinguistic Approach to the *Romancero del rey don Pedro*

A. Introduction

In general, the problem of linking grammatical structure with external circumstances has been overlooked in traditional *Romancero* grammar criticism. For example, the stylistic approach to the language of the *Romancero*, discussed in chapter 2 of this study, failed to note a connection between the syntax of a *romance* and the context within which it was performed. Other approaches (e.g., "Romancero," *architecture temporelle*) similarly ignored the topics of language as a context-dependent structure and the *Romancero* grammar as a medium through which the poetic and ideological legacies of different societies could be produced and reproduced.

On the other hand, a sociolinguistic approach to the language of the *Romancero*, as outlined in the previous chapter of this study, is a methodology which is faithful at once to the tradition "que vive en variantes" and to the *colectividad* that is a fundamental ingredient in *Romancero* production. It provides a way of discovering the functional nature of the grammar of the *romances* through a thorough examination of both the texts and their social, historical, and political framework.

In light of the connection proposed above between what has elsewhere been called the "remarkable" *Romancero* grammar (here, *evaluation*) and the fabric of the oral literary situation in which *romances* are produced and transmitted, the texts chosen for detailed consideration in this chapter are *romances* that were generated within a well-documented historical period. These texts are from the *Romancero del rey don Pedro,* a group of *romances noticieros* in which the hostilities between King Pedro I of Castile and his bastard brothers, the Trastámaras, emerged as focal points in the notorious *guerra civil romancística* of the fourteenth century. The texts that constitute this *Romancero* served as propaganda for both sides in the fratricidal struggle between the two brothers as well as in the ensuing years of strife between their descendants.

Three of the *romances* in the Pedro cycle deal with the death of doña Blanca, Pedro's wife, and the appearance of a prophetic shepherd who foresaw doom for the King as a result. The unhappy figure of the Queen, who was imprisoned by Pedro immediately following her marriage to him, and who died under uncertain circumstances two years later, became a rallying point for the Trastámarans. The texts generated by singers in their employ used her to point to Pedro's unfitness for the leadership of Castile. Pedro's supporters responded with a *romance* which accused Blanca of adultery, thus rationalizing the King's behavior towards her.

Each of the texts dealing with the death of doña Blanca and the *pastorcico profeta* demonstrates the use of evaluation in the *Romancero*. Evaluative devices account for much of the language in the *romances* and may be equated with the "remarkable" *Romancero* grammar commented on by the ballad critics discussed in chapter 2 of this study. It is interesting to note that in many of the texts of the *Romancero del rey don Pedro*, evaluation functions principally to reinterpret and reformulate events already known to the audience. The *romances* thus serve simply as a framework for the evaluation. They build on the information shared between the singer and the audience, defining for the listeners the attitudes they ought or ought not to take towards the events of the civil war. The anti-Pedro *romances* prescribed legitimization by the Castilian populace of the Trastámaran takeover. The texts sung by Pedro's supporters suggested the opposite posture.

It is probable that *romances noticieros* such as the texts of the *Romancero del rey don Pedro* were composed by *juglares* in the service of the court or the nobility and that they received payment for their partisan compositions.[1] This made the *romances* a deliberate tool in the shaping of public opinion— a phenomenon quite apparent in the linguistic maneuvers of the texts. But the fact that the *romances* were produced through a collaboration between official authorities and singers also resulted in what will later be seen as an interesting manipulation of customary and officially sanctioned doctrines within the mold of traditional discourse.[2] The principles of the *Siete Partidas,* for example, officially approved by King Pedro's father, Alfonso XI, became the premises for Pedro's judgement by the Trastámaran faction in the *romances* which slandered him.[3]

In addition to representing official rather than popular opinion, the *juglares* who composed the *Romancero del rey don Pedro* were capable of lending to their partisan texts an authoritative quality. This quality derived from the respect the *juglares* were accorded in medieval Spanish society—a respect which ironically allowed them to successfully transmit the partisan views of the official element to the public at large, where the *romances* could be further circulated. Interestingly, this respect was noted by writers during the Middle Ages and protested against, for it seemed that the testimony of the oral poets was held in greater esteem than that of the historians. As Menéndez Pidal notes:

> El arzobispo Toledano . . .
> menciona expresamente a los
> juglares, si bien para protestar,
> como historiador, contra el
> excesivo crédito que ellos
> tenían entre las gentes.
>
> (*Poesía juglaresca* 224)

In the present chapter of this study, all of the factors of the conditions under which the *Romancero del rey don Pedro* was produced and transmitted will be considered. A sociolinguistic approach to the language of the *Romancero* will then be taken in order to describe the function of the remarkable *Romancero* grammar within a specific social, historical, and political context.

B. Historical Background

The fourteenth century was a period of great political and social upheaval for Castile. It was a time of intense family hatred—so frenzied that it left its mark by involving all of Spain, as well as England and France, in a ruinous civil war. The fourteenth century also saw the spread of the Black Plague, and the violent disturbance of social and economic relationships that resulted from its devastation.[4]

The Castilian troubles reached a peak when King Alfonso XI died. Alfonso had had children with both his legal wife, María de Portugal, and his mistress, Leonor de Guzmán. One of the costs of this polygamous arrangement was the ambition of each mother to see her own offspring successful against the children of the other. Immediately following Alfonso's death, the antagonism between the two women peaked. María's son, Pedro, as Alfonso's only lawful child, ascended the throne in 1350. María, taking advantage of her son's new-found authority, wasted no time in securing her rival's imprisonment and ultimately, her execution. By definitively ending Leonor's presence in Castile, she expected to curtail the ambitions of her dead husband's mistress for his bastard children. As it turned out, the opposite result was obtained. Outraged by María's vengeful act and further inspired by the lingering memory of the mother who had died with the hope of seeing her own family replace Pedro on the Castilian throne, Leonor's sons, Enrique de Trastámara and Fadrique, Maestre de Santiago, embarked on a fratricidal struggle with Pedro that was to last until the King's death at Enrique's hands in 1369.

The conflict between the Trastámaran faction and King Pedro I was characterized chiefly by the kinship between the principal adversaries and the claim of legitimacy pronounced by each party.[5] Pedro was, by birth, Alfonso's legal heir. However, as has been noted by anthropologists:

> No system of succession is completely automatic. . . . In the first place, high office generally demands some particular qualities of its incumbents, even if only *mens sana in corpore sana.*[6]

According to some of his contemporaries, Pedro did not have the leadership qualities considered necessary for high office in Castile.[7] He was given to executing his enemies—or suspected enemies—and his policies presented a grave threat to some of the most prominent noble families in Europe.[8] Leonor's sons, on the other hand, were perceived by many as able leaders, and although others saw them as only little better than their half brother, they nevertheless supported the Trastámaras as the lesser of the two evils.[9]

Enrique de Trastámara, who after his brother Fadrique's death became the sole contender for Pedro's throne, was the descendant of both the former king, Alfonso XI, and the powerful noble family of Leonor de Guzmán. He had no strictly legal grounds on which to base his royal aspirations, but he did have the support of the Castilian nobility and of other European powers. He also had the popular approval of those who shared with him an unsympathetic attitude towards Jews and who blamed Pedro for the advancements made by this group under his rule (Froissart 1: 503; ch. 198).

Because Enrique was proclaimed by so many to be better qualified for the monarchy than his half brother Pedro and because he was in fact King Alfonso's son, his claim to the throne was considered legitimate (or at least capable of being legitimized) by some of the most influential families and individuals in Europe.[10] Indeed, as is generally the case, this factor became more important than any systematic rules of succession Castile may have had.[11] Force was the final arbiter in the struggle for power, and the choice of Enrique over Pedro was made through success in the civil war that followed the death of King Alfonso.

C. Legitimizing Trastámaran Rule

Because Enrique's rise to power bypassed the customary rules of legitimate birth and primogeniture, the Trastámaran faction had an imperative need to publicly insist upon its own legitimacy. The Trastámarans had to construct some justification for Enrique's position and to rationalize Pedro's demise. They were lucky in this respect, for their task was made simpler by Pedro himself, whose unfortunate marriage to Blanca de Borbón had resulted in an easy rallying point for his enemies.[1 2]

Queen Blanca, the daughter of the Duke of Bourbon, had been brought to Castile in 1353 by Juan Alfonso, lord of Albuquerque, who hoped to strengthen his hold over the King by arranging the marriage (O'Callaghan 420). Pedro married Blanca that year in Valladolid, but thereafter had nothing to do with her except to have her imprisoned until her death in 1361. In the meantime, the King kept the company of María de Padilla, with whom he had several children.

The King's actions towards his wife provided a convenient doctrine for those who sought to justify the Trastámaran success. Blanca's suffering and death inspired precisely the moral outrage that the usurpers needed in order to sanction their takeover. Blanca's circumstances also showed Pedro as an unsuitable king who violated the basic precepts for sovereignty set down in the *Siete Partidas*. These legal codes called for courtesy, respect, and above all, a sense of duty on the part of the monarch towards his wife.[1 3]

On the basis of these ready allegations against Pedro's monarchy, a group of ballads was composed. The purpose of these *romances noticieros* was to convert the story of Pedro's abandonment of Blanca into a popular and commonly accepted example of the King's inability to meet the requirements for Castilian leadership. In terms of fourteenth-century Castile, there was no better way to promote this partisan view. As Menéndez Pidal has commented, the *noticieros* "son para su tiempo el gran medio de publicidad, algo como el periodismo de entonces."[1 4] But equally important was the fact that the narrative framework of the *noticieros* spoke directly to the political needs of the Trastámaran group. The subtle manipulations of syntax and lexis permitted by the *Romancero* style were appropriated by the new powers in order to channel accusations and slander against Pedro into the popular currency. Because the *Romancero* is literature to which "it should not be possible for any adult, literate or not, to say, 'I do not understand it,' "[1 5] the *romances* were ideal as vehicles for the mass distribution of Trastámaran political propaganda. As popular literature, the *romances* passed into the public domain where their repeated singing functioned to reinforce a Trastámaran definition of legitimate rule. This new definition, based on a standard of behavior which overshadowed the customary rules of succession, was taken seriously by the people and soon became established in the community.[1 6] The disfranchised Trastámarans were thus able to clothe their actions with legitimacy, even daring to insinuate, in one of the ballads, that King Pedro himself was a bastard and therefore had no rightful claim to the throne in the first place.[1 7]

In response to the *romances* that supported the Trastámaran camp, Pedro's followers began to spread their own rumors through the same medium. As Menéndez y Pelayo has remarked:

Si en el campo de D. Enrique se mintió y calumnió a sabiendas, no es extraño, aunque sí doloroso, que lo mismo hiciesen los partidarios de D. Pedro que permanecieron fieles a su memoria y quisieron justificar hasta sus más atroces crueldades.[18]

Thus one finds *romances* used to justify both the victor and the vanquished in the fratricidal contest.

The *romances* spread by the Trastámarans projected an image of the deposed king as cruel and arrogant. They depicted his rule as a downward course which could have been checked had Pedro heeded the divine warnings he received. Deliberately designed to rationalize the state of affairs which existed following Pedro's demise, some of them specifically mentioned Enrique as the King's successor if Pedro did not listen to God and return to his abandoned wife.[19] Thus the *romances* lent the human choice of Enrique over Pedro the confirmation of divine authority. The *romances* also cited as fact the personal involvement of the malevolent Pedro in Blanca's death. Although this involvement has been contradicted by papal documents, it nevertheless has survived to the present day as evidence of the ideological legacy left by the medieval *romances*.[20]

The *romances* that justified the position the Trastámarans had won were probably composed shortly after Enrique came into power, and then modified through transmission to fit the molds of subsequent years of Trastámaran rule.[21] By sorting out the political and historical structures around which fourteenth-century Castilian society was organized, it is possible to make some progress towards understanding the role played by them in the legitimization of Enrique and his descendants. The following sections of this chapter consider six texts from the *Romancero del rey don Pedro*[22] against this backdrop, discussing evaluation in the *romances* in terms of the turbulence of fourteenth-century Castilian politics.

D. A Sociolinguistic Approach to the *Romancero del rey don Pedro*

In the previous chapter, the far-reaching use of some evaluative devices in the *Romancero* was discussed. The purpose of the current chapter is to show that these same, or very similar, evaluative devices were used in a like manner by the singers of the *Romancero del rey don Pedro*. These singers, who were employed by partisan patrons, worked hand-in-glove with the attitudes and beliefs of their audiences in order to set new conditions for legitimate rule in Castile, using the structure of the *Romancero* as a vehicle for their ideological mission. Similarly, the singers of the *romances* that supported King Pedro's rule structured their defense around the characteristic patternings of *Romancero* language.

1. The *Romance de doña Blanca*

The first text to be discussed here is one of the few surviving *romances* supportive of the dethroned king.[23] It concerns the abandonment of Queen Blanca by Pedro, but it uses a novel perspective to make a point which is ultimately favorable to the King. The *romance* argues that Blanca and Fadrique, Pedro's half brother, share an illegitimate child, and that this misadventure was the cause of Pedro's actions towards the two (Fadrique was murdered by Pedro). Each element in the text is planned so that it has the effect of furthering King Pedro's innocence, and Blanca and Fadrique's guilt. The text, numbered according to the *Primavera y flor de romances* as "67a," and a chart which details the course of evaluation in it, are given in table 2. The chart indicates both the distribution of evaluative devices and the grammatical classification of each individual clause (hemistichs, in the case of the *Romancero*). Each unit is grouped according to function under three general headings: Comparators, Correlatives, and Explicatives. The clauses are subdivided within the general headings in terms of the syntactic complexity they introduce into the narrative (e.g., Negative Clauses, Imperfect Clauses, Interrogative Clauses). Clauses contained within direct discourse passages are in italics.

The general argument of text 67a is that King Pedro's sanctions against his wife and half brother were precipitated by an illicit affair between the two. It is an argument that responded to a Trastámaran version of the events of Pedro's rule. This version, popularized through a group of *romances* (four of which will be discussed in this study) which pointed to the King as a wanton and ruthless murderer of innocent relatives, was apparently an accepted account of the King's relationship with his family. The singer of text 67a, for example, though firmly in Pedro's camp, does not even attempt to dispute the charges that Pedro was personally involved in his wife's murder (although this charge was in fact of dubious veracity). Rather, the singer reinterprets and reformulates the details of this involvement so as to reshape the Trastámaran slander into a statement condemnatory not of Pedro, but of his victims.

Text 67a was probably composed for the benefit of Pedro's descendants rather than for Pedro himself, for, as the text shows, Pedro had already been succeeded by the Trastámarans ("y como el rey don Enrique   reinase luego en Castilla" [37a-37b]) at the time of composition. It is likely that the singer of the text sought to invalidate the claim for legitimacy made in other *romances* by the Trastámaran faction through the justification of one of Pedro's most notorious deeds—i.e., the murder of Queen Blanca. It is probable that the singer also sought, in the *romance,* to uphold the rights of Pedro's family to the throne. The family, who was denied these rights as a result of the Trastámaran coup, could use the argument (suggested within the text

TABLE 2

Evaluative Clauses in the *Romance de la reina doña Blanca* (Text 67a)

	a	b
1	Entre las gentes se suena,	y no por cosa sabida,
2	que de ese buen Maestre	don Fadrique de Castilla
3	la reina estaba preñada;	otros dicen que parida.
4	No se sabe por de cierto,	mas el vulgo lo decía:
5	ellos piensan que es secreto,	ya esto no se escondía.
6	La reina con su . . .	por Alonso Pérez envía,
7	mandóle que viniese	de noche y no de día:
8	secretario es del Maestre,	en quien fiarse podía.
9	Cuando lo tuvo delante,	de esta manera decía:
10	—¿Adónde está el Maestre?	¿Qué es dél que no parecía?
11	¡Para ser de sangre real,	hecho ha gran villanía!
12	Ha deshonrado mi casa,	y dícese por Sevilla
13	que una de mis doncellas	del Maestre está parida.
14	—El Maestre, mi señora,	tiene cercada a Coimbra,
15	y si vuestra Alteza manda,	yo luego lo llamaría;
16	y sepa vuestra Alteza	que el Maestre no se escondía:
17	lo que vuestra Alteza dice,	debe ser muy gran mentira.
18	—No lo es, dijo la reina,	que yo te lo mostraría,—
19	Mandara sacar un niño	que en su palacio tenía:
20	sacólo su camarera	envuelto en una faldilla.
21	—Mira, mira, Alonso Pérez,	el niño, ¿a quién parecía?
22	—Al Maestre, mi señora,	Alonso Pérez decía.
23	—Pues daldo luego a criar,	y a nadie esto se diga.—
24	Sálese Alonso Pérez,	ya se sale de Sevilla;
25	muy triste queda la reina,	que consuelo no tenía;
26	llorando de los sus ojos,	de la su boca decía:
27	—Yo, desventurada reina,	más que cuantas son nacidas,
28	casáronme con el rey	por la desventura mía.
29	De la noche de la boda	nunca más visto lo había,
30	y su hermano el Maestre	me ha tenido en compañía.
31	Si esto ha pasado,	toda la culpa era mía.
32	Si el rey don Pedro lo sabe,	de ambos se vengaría;
33	mucho más de mí, la reina	por la mala suerte mía.—
34	Ya llegaba Alonso Pérez	a Llerena, aquesa villa:
35	puso el infante a criar	en poder de una judía;
36	criada fue del Maestre,	Paloma por nombre había;
37	y como el rey don Enrique	reinase luego en Castilla,
38	tomara aquel infante	y almirante lo hacía:
39	hijo era de su hermano	como el romance decía.

Source for text 67a: Menéndez y Pelayo, *Antología de poetas líricos castellanos* 8: 131-33.

Continued on next page

Table 2–*Continued*

Comparators	Correlatives	Explicatives
Negative Clauses:	**Present Perfect Clauses:**	1b y no por cosa sabida
1b y no por cosa sabida[a]	12a *Ha deshonrado mi casa*	28b *por la desventura mía*
4a No se sabe por de cierto	30b *me ha tenido en*	33b *por la mala suerte mía*
5b ya esto no se escondía	*compañía*	36a- criada fue del Maestre
7b de noche y no de día		36b Paloma por nombre
10b *¿Qué es dél que no*	**Present Tense Clauses:**	había
parecía?	1a Entre las gentes se suena	37a- y como el rey don
16b *que el Maestre no se*	3b otros dicen que parida	Enrique
escondía	4a No se sabe por de cierto	37b reinase luego en Castilla
18a *No lo es*	5a ellos piensan que es	
25b que consuelo no tenía	secreto	
	8a secretario es del Maestre	
Si **Clauses:**	10a- *¿Adónde está el*	
15a- *y si vuestra Alteza*	*Maestre?*	
manda	10b *¿Qué es dél que no*	
15b *yo luego lo llamaría*	*parecía?*	
31a- *Si esto ha pasado*	12b *y dícese por Sevilla*	
31b *toda la culpa era mía*	13b *del Maestre está parida*	
32a- *Si el rey don Pedro*	14b *tiene cercada a Coimbra*	
lo sabe	17a- *lo que vuestra Alteza*	
32b *de ambos se vengaría*	*dice*	
	17b *debe ser muy gran*	
Subjunctive Clauses:	*mentira*	
7a mandóle que viniese	18a *No lo es*	
	24a- Sálese Alonso Pérez	
Imperative Clauses:	24b ya se sale de Sevilla	
16a *y sepa vuestra Alteza*	25a muy triste queda la	
21a *Mira, mira, Alonso Pérez*	reina	
23a- *Pues daldo luego a criar*		
23b *y a nadie esto se diga*	**Imperfect Clauses:**	
	3a la reina estaba preñada	
Interrogative Clauses:	4b mas el vulgo lo decía	
10a- *¿Adónde está el*	5b ya esto no se escondía	
Maestre?	6b por Alonso Pérez envía	
10b *¿Qué es dél que no*	8b en quien fiarse podía	
parecía?	9b de esta manera decía	
21b *el niño, ¿a quién*	10b *¿Qué es dél que no*	
parecía?	*parecía?*	

Continued on next page

Table 2–*Continued*

Comparators–*Continued*	Correlatives–*Continued*	Explicatives–*Continued*
Conditional Clauses:	**Imperfect Clauses–***Continued***:**	
18b *que yo te lo mostraría*	16b *que el Maestre no se*	
	escondía	
	21b *el niño, ¿a quién*	
	parecía?	
	22b Alonso Pérez decía	
	25b que consuelo no tenía	
	26b de la su boca decía	
	34a Ya llegaba Alonso Pérez	
	36b Paloma por nombre	
	había	
	38b y almirante lo hacía	
	39a- hijo era de su hermano	
	39b como el romance decía	
	Progressive Clauses:	
	26a llorando de los sus ojos	
	Attributives:	
	2a- que de ese buen	
	Maestre	
	2b don Fadrique de Castilla	
	17b *debe ser muy gran*	
	mentira	
	Appositives:	
	27a *Yo, desventurada reina*	
	34b a Llerena, aquesa villa	

a The thrust of the Labovian method is clause-based, and in this table, each hemistich of the *romance* is, for the most part, treated as a narrative clause. In some cases, it seems that the clauses have more than one evaluative function. When this occurs, the clause is listed more than once in the table–e.g., "y no por cosa sabida" (1b) is both a negative clause functioning as a comparator and an explicative.

Note: clauses contained within direct discourse passages are in italics.

of the *romance*) that Pedro was only exercising his prerogative as husband to defend his household against adultery when he ordered Blanca's and Fadrique's deaths.

The argument developed through the verses of the *romance* places the composition within the context of the Galician wars, at which time Pedro's son-in-law, the Duke of Lancaster, was attempting to wrest control from Juan I, Enrique de Trastámara's son. The singer of the *romance,* who presupposes the audience's knowledge of the various mechanisms by which the Trastámarans came to power and Pedro was dethroned, uses the text not to report the details of these mechanisms, but rather, as a framework for their evaluation. Its structure thus draws upon what Labov has called, "a cognitive background considerably richer than the set of events observed,"[24] presuming as it does that the audience has certain preconceived attitudes towards the political conflicts of the time. Calling upon almost every grammatical resource in the Spanish language, the singer of text 67a endeavors to reverse the Trastámaran charges against the dethroned king and redirect the sympathies of the audience towards the family of the leader they earlier shunned.

Text 67a begins with an Abstract (1a-3b) which effectively summarizes the argument presented in the *romance*—that is to say, the treachery of Blanca and Fadrique against the house of King Pedro. Because the Abstract contains the names of the personalities on whom the story rests, it also serves as part of the Orientation. The names, "Blanca" and "Fadrique," locate the listeners within the fabric of the fratricidal struggle between Pedro and his brothers as well as the disaffection between the King and his wife. They recall to the audience the details of a story which is already familiar to them—that is, the death of this pair at Pedro's hands.

The Abstract/Orientation section of the text is followed by a short evaluation (4a-5b) in which the singer insists upon the secretive aspect of the text's contents and indicates to the audience that those who listen will be privy to a heretofore concealed scandal. The singer also disclaims authority in these opening lines, refusing to bear responsibility for the details of the story and begging to be exonerated from the nasty deed of blackening a woman's reputation.

In addition to evaluating the Abstract of the text, lines 4a-5b contain further orienting material. As the discussion of verbal tenses will show, this section, as well as lines 6a-9b, places the listeners in the midst of certain ongoing circumstances, orienting them *within* the *romance* with respect to events that were happening prior to its Complicating Action, and *outside* of the *romance* with respect to current activities in the conflict-ridden society. The text is thus structured so that the first lines leave the audience in attentive anticipation of the plot sequence which unfolds in the Complicating Action (6a-26b).

The Complicating Action section of the *romance* begins as the Queen, faced with the consequences of her misdeed, contracts to have the child she shares with Fadrique secretly taken away. The *romance* spells out the details of this enterprise, using dialogue as a vehicle through which the plot is both furthered and evaluated. However, the true Evaluation section of the text does not occur until after the completion of the Complicating Action. In lines 27a-33b, the Queen, in a flashback which is presented as an "aside" to the audience, delivers a soliloquy which functions as an evaluation of the entire situation. King Pedro is introduced into the text of the *romance*, and the suggestion of his certain revenge on the surreptitious lovers points to the justification of his involvement in the deaths of his wife and half brother.

The Resolution of the *romance*'s plot lies outside of the text. It is the punishment of doña Blanca and Fadrique for their adulterous affair—that is to say, their death at Pedro's behest. The Coda (34a-36b) brings the audience up-to-date with the information that the bastard child was taken by Fadrique's secretary to be brought up in a Jewish home. An additional three lines in the *romance* seem to have been added by a later singer for the benefit of the Almirante de Castilla family, a point which will be taken up in section 4D2 of this study.

As in the *Romance de la morilla burlada* discussed in chapters 2 and 3 of this study, evaluative devices in text 67a are not confined solely to the Evaluation section. They are instead present throughout the text as mechanisms through which the audience is guided according to the predispositions of the singer. For example, comparators in the first thirteen lines of the work provide the singer with the means to repeatedly suggest, or hint at, situations of which no certain knowledge is otherwise claimed. As may be recalled, comparators perform the evaluative role of comparing actions that are explicitly stated to have occurred with those that are not. In text 67a, negative clauses, functioning as comparators, serve the dual purpose of allowing the singer to be frank with the audience (e.g., the singer admits that of the Queen's pregnancy, "no se sabe por de cierto" [4a]) as they skillfully bring to the fore unsubstantiated rumors (these rumors, through their very verbalization, are lent a certain credibility). A similar effect is obtained when the liaison between Blanca and Fadrique is said to be known "no por cosa sabida" (1b), while the lines "que de ese buen Maestre   don Fadrique de Castilla / la reina estaba preñada" (2a-3a) stand alone as an affirmative statement. In a like use of the negative, Fadrique is described in terms of actions he did *not* take. "¿Qué es dél que no parecía?" (10b), the Queen asks, hinting through the negative particle that Fadrique is hiding. "Que el Maestre no se escondía," (16b), Fadrique's secretary answers, correctly interpreting the Queen's suspicions and confirming for the audience, which already knows from the Abstract of the illicit affair, the notion that Fadrique must indeed have fled in cowardice.

Like the negative clauses, interrogative clauses function as suggestions of the existence of circumstances and situations that are not explicitly stated. When Blanca asks Alonso Pérez, "¿Adónde está el Maestre?   ¿Qué es dél que no parecía?" (10a-10b), she is inquiring about events that are unknown to her. Effectively, however, she is presupposing that Fadrique has secretly left her household. But the interrogative, unlike the negative, begs an action or response. The Queen's questioning of Fadrique's secretary carries an implicit threat of negative consequences if no response is given or action taken. The audience, with foreknowledge of Pedro's treatment of his wife and half brother, keenly perceives the threat. So does the secretary, who responds by agreeing to hide the child.

The imperative also has the force of implying negative consequences. The Queen warns Alonso Pérez, for example, "y a nadie esto se diga" (23b), referring similarly to the expected vengeance of the King if he were to become aware of the treachery.

Si clauses and conditional/subjunctive constructions are perhaps the forms *par excellence* through which suggestions of unrealized events or actions may be made. These clauses are found throughout the *romance* (e.g., 15a-15b, 18b, and 31a-32b), and they allow various situations to be alluded to in terms of what would, or will, happen if other conditions are, or are not, met. Here, unlike the case of other comparators, the consequences are spelled out. Line 32a-32b of the Queen's soliloquy provides an archetypal example of this use of the conditional: "Si el rey don Pedro lo sabe,   de ambos se vengaría," she says, making concrete the thrust of the story.

Other syntactic constructions used in text 67a contribute to the evaluative stance of the *romance* in a less obvious manner. The correlative category of syntactically complex clauses, for example, includes the problematic imperfect in its catalogue of evaluative devices. The imperfect, which has traditionally been the most troublesome aspect of the *Romancero* grammar, becomes a principal evaluator within a sociolinguistic framework.

Imperfect clauses function in the text to bring together a wide range of simultaneous events. As correlatives, they suspend the action of the *romance* while the listeners await the consequences of the situations described. These consequences, as a result, are highlighted. Outstanding examples of such use of imperfect clauses in text 67a can be seen in 3a, 4b, 5b, 6b, 8b, and 9b. The imperfect here orients the listener within an ongoing set of circumstances while it carries the evaluative force of setting the stage for the confrontation between doña Blanca and Alonso Pérez. It has the effect of building up a certain suspense while it accumulates an assortment of contemporaneous activities: the Queen was giving birth; the people were gossiping; the birth was being concealed; the Queen was sending for Alonso Pérez. By using the imperfect, the singer brings together a set of actions and events that dangle in mid-air until the dialogue, which constitutes the Complicating Action of the *romance,* begins.

It should be noted that even at the very point at which the Complicating Action is about to be presented by the singer, the imperfect is used. Many critics (e.g., Lenz[25] and Szertics[26]) have maintained that the imperfect is often employed, like the preterite, as a narrative tense.[27] But the deliberate use of the imperfect in the introduction of the dialogue (e.g., *decía* in 9b and 26b) indicates that the form may be used also for the purposes of priming the audience for the action which follows. The multiple imperfect forms serve the purpose of suspending the action in the *romance* while the audience waits, as Labov has put it, "for the other shoe to fall" (388).

Like the imperfect, present tense clauses also function as correlatives, suspending the action of the *romance* while positioning the audience. But present tense clauses have a special function in the *Romancero*: they serve to situate the listener *within* the *Romancero* text itself. As Michèle Débax (mentioned earlier as a proponent of *architecture temporelle*) has written, this aspect of the temporal architecture of a *romance* "implique donc que l'évènement relaté est contemporain de l'énonciation."[28] Certain actions (e.g., gossiping [1a, 3b, and 5a]) and circumstances (e.g., "secretario es del Maestre" [8a]) are said to be in force as the *romance* is sung. The listener, who is an integral part of the oral literary situation of the text, becomes part of its action as well, for the evolution of the *romance* is as immediate as its performance. The audience becomes the *gente* of 5a, waiting to pass judgement on the Queen and Fadrique. Later on in the text, it "watches" as Alonso Pérez departs with the evidence of the pair's misconduct (24a and 24b), leaving the sad and guilty Queen behind (25a).

Szertics alludes to this property of the present tense in his study, stating that it functions to actualize and dramatize certain events (64). The fact remains, however, that this narrative use of the present tense is a subtle maneuver through which the singer of the *romance* relates the "present" of the text to the "present" of the performance. The result is that the audience becomes engaged in the action of the *romance,* which means, in text 67a, that its status as listener is transformed into that of participant. This transformation is particularly effective as an evaluative device in that it has the pretense of giving the audience the opportunity to makes its own decision on the evidence presented by the singer. In fact, judgement of the Queen and Fadrique is made within the text itself. But by positive identification between the listeners and the *gente* of the *romance,* the singer leads the audience to agree with this judgement. Furthermore, as remarks that aid in building up anticipation for the Complicating Action of the *romance,* the evaluative force of *dicen que* is far greater than *dijo que.* The sense of urgency to find out just *what* they are saying outweighs the level of anticipation encouraged by the preterite tense. The same idea of ongoing debate and questioning introduced by the "unfinished" aspect of the imperfect exists in the use of the present.

In sum, the alternation of imperfect and present forms in the first nine lines of text 67a provides the singer with a subtle technique through which the audience can be induced to participate in the evaluative stance of the *romance*. This technique may well result in an impression of "close-up" and distancing akin to the art of cinematography, as suggested by Menéndez Pidal and others, but even in film, the method is linked to more than stylistics alone.

Dialogue is another evaluative device which plays an important part in guiding the listeners through the argument of the text. The interview between Blanca and Alonso Pérez, for example, which begins in 10a, preeminently substantiates the innuendo of the first lines of the work, giving the impression that the protagonists are voicing their own indictment. There is a diversity of verbal tense and aspect in this section of the text, as there was in the first nine lines, but in some respects, this diversity responds to a slightly different evaluative purpose. The dialogue between Blanca and Alonso Pérez follows certain conversational rules which, as was noted in chapter 2, diverge from the sequence of tenses expected in third person narration.

Focusing specifically on the verbal exchange between the Queen and the secretary, one can identify the various syntactic and semantic strategies used by the "speakers" to evaluate the situation that is being described. The Queen is in control of the conversation. She makes certain demands of Alonso Pérez, to which he must reply in kind. Using a system of verbal tense and aspect that relates back to points made much earlier in the *romance* (e.g., the Abstract), she transfers the attention of the listener backward and forward in time, orienting and *reorienting* the audience within the set of circumstances which ultimately lead to Pedro's revenge. The result is that the listeners both receive the long-anticipated answer to the question of what happened in the interview between Alonso Pérez and Blanca that gave rise to the Abstract, and acquire some of the evaluative information about the illicit lovers that implies justification of Pedro's involvement in their deaths.

It is interesting to note that through the use of such evaluative devices as comparators and correlatives in the dialogue, the most damning characterization made is that of Fadrique, who is absent from the interview. The special properties of dialogue that, through evaluative clauses, allow a judgement to be made of events not explicitly stated in the *romance,* is made clear in the text. Fadrique is not given an opportunity to "speak for himself" in the *romance,* but the listener knows, both through his very absence, and through questions and demands put to his secretary by the Queen, as well as the secretary's responses, that he is a coward who cannot face up to his own misdeeds. He is, further, a blight upon the royal blood of his—and Pedro's—father, which also suggests justification for the King's actions against him. But the portrayal of the Queen through her utterances in the dialogue is no better. She neither admits to her participation in the misdeed nor accepts its consequences. Rather, she is heard by the audience demanding the aid of the faithful secretary in the concealment of the child.

In the Evaluation section which follows shortly after the dialogue ends (27a), the singer makes plain the point of the story of text 67a. This is not simply to condemn the Queen and Fadrique for their adulterous affair, but to justify what the audience knows to be the terrible revenge taken by Pedro on them. What the *romance* has hitherto hinted at is here made explicit. In a correlative clause (27a-27b) used to heighten the effect of the description (the case here is of a double appositive and a comparative), Blanca identifies herself to the audience as ". . . desventurada . . .   más que cuantas son nacidas" (27a-27b). She then explains this self-characterization through an explicative, "por la desventura mía" (28b), which refers the listener to her marriage to King Pedro. She continues the explanation by noting the King's abandonment of her after the wedding and the subsequent solace she found in the company of his half brother (29a-30b). The use of the past perfect (*había visto*) to describe the Queen's relationship with Pedro as opposed to the present perfect (*ha tenido*) in the liaison with Fadrique conveniently parallels the difference between the two situations. The past perfect is the form used to indicate a completed action from a past point of view. The Queen looks back on her marriage to Pedro and comments on its termination immediately after the nuptial vows. The present perfect form, on the other hand, indicates a past action which bears a relation to the present. The *compañía* (30b) that the Maestre had with the Queen has resulted in the circumstances in which Blanca now finds herself.

In the last lines of Blanca's soliloquy, the rationale for the story is unequivocally expressed. In a conditional statement, the Queen introduces the idea that Pedro now knows about the adultery and, using a conditional clause, she suggests the possibility of his vengeance (32b). Then, in an explicative, she laments her fate ("por la mala suerte mía"), claiming that her punishment will be even worse than Fadrique's (33a-33b).

The seven lines discussed above are bound together by the singer of the *romance*'s evaluation of one of the most notorious events of King Pedro's rule: the death of doña Blanca. The grammatical features of the section aid the singer in allowing the Queen to argue her own case before the audience, presenting to them the mitigating circumstances in which her adulterous affair took place, yet guiding them, through the lexis and syntax of the soliloquy, in a negative evaluation of the situation. Blanca, who calls herself *desventurada,* is in fact guilty of adultery, and her fate, expressed in tandem with the close of her soliloquy, is to be punished by the King.

The remainder of text 67a brings the audience up-to-date in a narrative statement of the outcome of Alonso Pérez's journey and his final destination in the project of hiding from Pedro the child of Blanca and Fadrique (34a-35b). The Resolution of the text's action, on the other hand, lies outside of the text itself. This Resolution was, as the audience well knew, the deaths of doña Blanca and her lover, Fadrique.

The last three lines of the text seem to introduce an unexpected new theme into the *romance*. This theme deals with Fadrique's child, upon whom Enrique conferred admiralty. It is likely that these lines were added to the *romance* during transmission, for they seem to belong more to the argument of later compositions than to that of text 67a. These later compositions reworked the story of Blanca and Fadrique's adultery into a claim for royal and "pure" blood on the part of the powerful Almirante de Castilla family, of which Alonso Enríquez, Fadrique's bastard son, was progenitor. The following section of this study will take up the notion of text 67a's reformulation for different evaluative purposes.

On the basis of the study of evaluation in the verses of text 67a, the conclusion may be reached that the syntactic complexities introduced into a *romance* by comparators, correlatives, and explicatives cannot be attributed to stylistic interests alone. Rather, these complexities contribute in a calculated way to the evaluative posture of a composition. This point will be further explored and elaborated on in five texts that defend Trastámaran rule: 67, 66, 66a, 68, and 68a, as numbered in the *Primavera y flor de romances*.

2. The *Romance de doña Blanca* (Text 67)

Romances noticieros like text 67a use the *Romancero* as a forum for making political statements. The *Romancero,* as a popular art form, lends itself particularly well to this type of employment. But it must be remembered that the *Romancero* does not function as a single-directioned vehicle for the predispositions of the singer. The shape of a *romance* responds also to the tendencies of the audience for whom it is performed. The relationship of this factor to the question of the *Romancero*'s remarkable grammar is as follows: each composition or version of a *romance* uses different syntactic and lexical devices according to the demeanor of its interlocutors. One text's narrative may become another's dialogue in the interests of evaluating a situation before different audiences. Similarly, verbal tense and aspect may be changed and lexis redefined.

The changes that may occur in the language of the *romances* during the transmission of a text are precisely the factors involved in the "new" grammar found in a different version of text 67a. Text 67, "Entre la gente se dice," is a basic reworking of the theme of the previous text. This *romance,* however, responds not so much to the concerns of an audience which took as fact Pedro's ruthless dealings with his enemies, but rather to the preoccupations of a later group among whom a disgrace in one of Castile's most powerful families was rumored.

Text 67 is a composition which rehearses the events of an earlier *romance* so that it may then evaluate these events to its own advantage. The work and its evaluation chart appear in table 3.

Text 67 follows the basic pattern of 67a in its opening sections. It begins with a four-line (1a-4b) Abstract-cum-Orientation which both summarizes the story (Blanca's reputed adultery with Fadrique) and identifies some of the *romance*'s protagonists (Blanca, Fadrique, and Pedro), as well as the situation in which they find themselves. In a short Evaluation which follows (5a-6b), the notion of the secretive nature of the information given in the Abstract is elaborated. This theme continues in 7a-13b in which the thread of the Abstract is pursued (the idea of Pedro's revenge is introduced) and the listeners are prepared for the action of the narrative with additional orienting material (Pedro is far away; the Queen is summoning aid from Fadrique's secretary).

The Complicating Action section (14a-25b) consists of a dialogue between Blanca and Alonso Pérez which recapitulates the course of events foreshadowed in the Abstract. The Queen discusses with the secretary her thinly veiled treachery (she claims the child's mother is an *hermana de leche* [22a]) and enlists his help in keeping the adultery a secret from Pedro. The Complicating Action is then resolved when Blanca entrusts the child to Alonso Pérez, who carries it off to Andalusia (26a-29b). Finally, a tense change brings the story up-to-date in a Coda (30a-32b). This section contains some general observations on the outcome of events (Blanca's child is brought up by Paloma, the daughter of a *linda judía* and a *tornadizo* [31a-32b]), but more importantly, it effectively pushes away and seals off the sequence of Complicating Actions described in the first half of the *romance*. The reasons for this somewhat surprising verbal maneuver are inherent in the text's evaluative strategy.

As noted earlier, the primary purpose of text 67 was to evaluate the information given in 67a. The first half of the text, therefore, repeats the earlier *romance* so as to remind the listeners of the "facts" of the situation. These facts may have been unfamiliar to the audience of the present *romance,* for the subversive anti-Trastámaran propaganda of text 67a was probably stifled by the post-Pedro rulers of Castile.[29] The singer of the new version may thus have thought to at once recall and re-establish the adultery of text 67a through a rehearsal of its details.

The next step in the singer's evaluative strategy was to restructure the narrative of the prior text so as to assert its tellability within a new oral literary situation. The new situation was that of the religiously charged fifteenth century during which the issue of *pureza de sangre* became a central and recurring theme in social and political practices.[30] The dynamic which made the new *romance* tellable within this religious context was the claim—made through the singer's assertion of adultery between Blanca and Fadrique—that the powerful Almirante de Castilla family, headed by Fadrique's bastard son, an ancestor of Fernando, *el rey católico*—descended maternally as well as paternally from royal and Catholic blood. This assertion was crucial, for the

TABLE 3

Evaluative Clauses in the *Romance que dice: "Entre la gente se dice"* (Text 67)

	a	b
1	Entre la gente se dice,	y no por cosa sabida,
2	que del honrado Maestre	don Fadrique de Castilla,
3	hermano del rey don Pedro	que por nombre el Cruel había,
4	está la reina preñada;	otros dicen que paría.
5	Entre los unos secreto,	entre otros se publica;
6	no se sabe por más cierto	de que el vulgo lo decía.
7	El rey don Pedro está lejos,	y de esto nada sabía.
8	que si de esto algo supiera,	bien castigado lo habría.
9	La reina, de muy turbada,	no sabe lo que haría
10	a la disfamia tan fuerte	que su casa padecía,
11	llamando a un secretario	que el Maestre bien quería;
12	Alonso Pérez se llama,	este es su nombre de pila;
13	desque lo tuvo delante,	estas palabras decía:
14	—Ven acá tú, Alonso Pérez,	dime verdad por mi vida:
15	¿qué es del honrado Maestre?	¿qué es dél, que no parecía?
16	—A caza es ido, señora,	con toda su montería.
17	—Dime, ¿qué te parece	de lo que dél se decía?
18	Quejosa estoy del Maestre	con gran razón que tenía,
19	por ser de sangre real,	y hacer tal villanía,
20	que dentro en mis palacios	una doncella paría,
21	de todas las de mi casa	a quien yo muy más quería;
22	mi hermana era de leche,	que negar no la podía.
23	A la ánima me llegara,	si en el reino se sabía.—
24	Alonso Pérez responde,	bien oiréis lo que decía
25	—Darme el nacido, señora,	que yo me lo criaría.—
26	Luego lo mandara dar	envuelto en una faldilla
27	amarilla y encarnada,	que guarnición no tenía.
28	Allá le lleva a criar	dentro del Andalucía,
29	a un lugar muy nombrado	que Llerena se decía.
30	A una ama le ha encargado;	hermosa es a maravilla,
31	Paloma tiene por nombre,	según se dice por la villa;
32	hija es de un tornadizo	y de una linda judía.
33	Mientra se cría el infante	sábelo doña María;
34	aquella falsa traidora	que los reinos revolvía.

Continued on next page

Table 3—*Continued*

a	b
	a	b
35	No estaba bien informada	cuando al rey se lo escribía:
36	—Yo, tu leal servidora,	doña María de Padilla,
37	que no te hice traición,	ni consentir la quería,
38	para que sepas, soy cierta	de aquesto te avisaría;
39	quien te la hace, señor,	declarar no se sufría,
40	hasta que venga a tiempo	que de mí a ti se diría.
41	No me alargo más, señor,	en aquesta letra mía.—
42	El rey, vista la presente,	que escribe doña María,
43	entró en consejo de aquesto	un lunes ¡qué fuerte día!
44	dejando por sustituto	en el cargo que tenía
45	en Tarifa la nombrada	los que aquí se nombrarían:
46	a don Fadrique de Acuña,	que es hombre de gran valía,
47	porque era sabio en la guerra	y en campo muy bien regía,
48	y a otro, su primo hermano	don García de Padilla,
49	y al buen Tello de Guzmán,	que el rey criado había,
50	el cual nombraban su ayo,	y él por tal le obedecía.
51	Un miércoles en la tarde	el rey tomaba la vía
52	con García López Osorio,	de quien sus secretos fía.
53	Llegado han aquella noche	a las puertas de Sevilla;
54	las puertas halló cerradas,	no sabe por do entraría,
55	sino por un muladar	que cabe el muro yacía.
56	El rey arrima el caballo,	subióse sobre la silla,
57	asido se ha de una almena,	en la ciudad se metía.
58	Fuese para sus palacios,	donde posarse solía:
59	ansí llamaba a la puerta	como si fuera de día.
60	Las guardas están velando,	muy muchas piedras le tiran:
61	herido han al rey don Pedro	de una mala herida.
62	Garci-López les da voces,	que estas palabras decía:
63	—Tate, tate, que es el rey	este que llegado había.—
64	Entonces bajan las guardas	por ver si verdad sería.
65	Abierto le han las puertas,	para su aposento aguija.
66	Tres días está secreto,	que no sale por la villa;
67	otro día escribió cartas:	a Cáliz aquesa villa,
68	al Maestre su hermano,	en las cuales le decía
69	que viniese a los torneos	que en Sevilla se hacían.

Source for text 67: Menéndez y Pelayo, *Antología de poetas líricos castellanos* 8: 129-31.

Continued on next page

Table 3—*Continued*

Comparators	Correlatives	Explicatives
Negative Clauses:	**Present Perfect Clauses:**	11b que el Maestre bien
1b y no por cosa sabida	30a A una ama le ha	quería
6a no se sabe por más	encargado	12b este es su nombre de pila
cierto	53a Llegado han aquella	18b *con gran razón que tenía*
7b y de esto nada sabía	noche	19a- *por ser de sangre real*
9b no sabe lo que haría	57a asido se ha de una	19b *y hacer tal villanía*
22b que negar no la podía	almena	27b que guarnición no tenía
27b que guarnición no tenía	61a herido han al rey	29b que Llerena se decía
35a No estaba bien		46b que es hombre de gran
informada	**Present Tense Clauses:**	valía
37a- *que no te hice traición*	1a Entre la gente se dice	47a- porque era sabio en la
37b *ni consentir la quería*	4a- está la reina preñada	guerra
54b no sabe por do entraría	4b otros dicen que paría	47b y en campo muy bien
55a sino por un muladar	5b entre otros se publica	regía
66b que no sale por la villa	6a no se sabe por más	49b que el rey criado había
	cierto	52b de quien sus secretos fía
Future Clauses:	7a El rey don Pedro está	59b como si fuera de día
24b bien oiréis lo que decía	lejos	61b de una mala herida
	12a Alonso Pérez se llama	64b por ver si verdad sería
Si **Clauses:**	24a Alonso Pérez responde	
8a- que si de esto algo	28a Allá le lleva a criar	
supiera	30b hermosa es a maravilla	
8b bien castigado lo habría	31a- Paloma tiene por	
23a- *A la ánima me llegara*	nombre	
23b *si en el reino se sabía*	31b según se dice por la villa	
59b como si fuera de día	32a hija es de un tornadizo	
64b por ver si verdad sería	33a- Mientra se cría el infante	
	33b sábelo doña María	
Subjunctive Clauses:	41a No me alargo más, señor	
40a hasta que venga a tiempo	42b que escribe doña María	
69a que viniese á los torneos	54b no sabe por do entraría	
	56a El rey arrima el caballo	
Imperative Clauses:	60b muy muchas piedras le	
14a- *Ven acá tú, Alonso*	tiran	
Pérez	62a Garci-López les da voces	

Continued on next page

Table 3—*Continued*

Comparators—*Continued*	Correlatives—*Continued*	Explicatives—*Continued*
Imperative Clauses— *Continued*:	**Present Tense Clauses—** *Continued*:	
14b *dime verdad por mi vida*	64a Entonces bajan las guardas	
17a *Dime, ¿qué te parece?*	65b para su aposento aguija	
25a *Darme el nacido, señora*	66a- Tres días está secreto	
63a *Tate, tate, que es el rey*	66b que no sale por la villa	

Imperfect Clauses:
4b otros dicen que paría
6b de que el vulgo lo decía
7b y de esto nada sabía
10b que su casa padecía
13b estas palabras decía
20b *una doncella paría*
21b *a quien yo muy más quería*
22a- *Mi hermana era de leche*
22b *que negar no la podía*
34b que los reinos revolvía
35a- No estaba bien informada
35b cuando al rey se lo escribía
44b en el cargo que tenía

Past Perfect Clauses:
63b este que llegado había

Note: clauses contained within direct discourse passages are in italics.

identity of the bastard child's mother had never been publicly revealed, and the well-known fact that the sire of such a prominent family had been brought up in a Jewish home invited slander and accusations against family members.

The singer of text 67 uses various devices to respond within the text of the *romance* to the sociopolitical situation which demanded "purity" in the ancestry of its leaders. First of all, the singer sets forth the situation in which Blanca seeks to hide the issue of her adulterous affair with Fadrique. This establishes the parentage of the bastard child and also accounts for the fact that Fadrique's son was brought up by a Jewish woman. However, because the point of the *romance* is no longer the justification and defense of King Pedro (as it was in text 67a), certain modifications are introduced in the evaluation of the protagonists and their activities to conform to the now pro-Trastámaran context. For example, Fadrique, the child's father, is characterized in a double attributive as the ". . . honrado Maestre   don Fadrique de Castilla" (2a-2b), while his half brother, Pedro, is explained in the clause that immediately follows as the one "que por nombre el Cruel había" (3b). This sequence of clauses invites a quick comparison of the two men, with the conclusion that of the two, Pedro is the less appealing.[31]

A second significant modification in the new version of the *romance* is that, whereas in the pro-Pedro text, the King's expected vengeance is introduced in order to evaluate the resolution of the events of the *romance*–i.e., the death of doña Blanca at Pedro's behest (known outside the text by the audience)–in text 67, the suggestion of Pedro's vengeance comes early, and serves to evaluate for the listeners not Blanca's, but Fadrique's death. Fadrique is the one who will ultimately be shown as the target of *el Cruel*'s wrath; Blanca is brought into the work simply for the purposes of establishing the identity of the bastard child's mother.

A third modification made in the text for the purposes of telling the story of text 67a within a context favorable to the Trastámaran family is found in the presentation of Paloma, the child's adoptive mother. The singer of the new text cannot deny the woman's Jewish heritage; this apparently has already been accepted as fact by the audience. On the other hand, the singer can–and does–manipulate audience sympathy by explaining in a ritual utterance, "hermosa es a maravilla" (30b), that this Jewish woman was exceptional. Furthermore, the singer explains, Paloma was really only part Jewish, for her father was *un tornadizo* (32a).

In addition to repeating the tale of adultery between Fadrique and Queen Blanca for the purposes of establishing the "pure" ancestry of the Almirante de Castilla family, text 67 tells a new story which confirms for the audience the legitimacy of Trastámaran family rule and the right of that family to have rid Castille of its former king.

According to custom[32] and to various precepts set forth in the codes of the *Siete Partidas*,[33] sovereignty gave to one person in Castile the charge and responsibility of seeing that justice was accomplished in civil society. These precepts allowed a king the authority to rule, but this authority was informed and checked by the goals for which it was established.[34] Hereditary succession thus did not preclude the idea that subjects could remind the king of his deficiencies with respect to his monarchal duties, and could, failing an appropriate response, forcibly remove him from his throne.

If the literature of the Spanish Renaissance can be considered as in any way reflective of the opinions held by the Castilians of the earlier period, this solution to the rule of an unjust king was taken for granted by the people. Gómez Manrique, for example, writes in his work *Regimiento de príncipes*:

> Ca no vos demandarán
> Cuenta de los que rezays
> No si vos disciplinays
> Non vos lo preguntaran . . .
> Si los culpados punistes
> O los malos consentistes
> desto sera la quistion.[35]

Guillén de Castro reiterates this idea in the seventeenth-century play *Amor constante*:

> Rey: ¿y es razón que muera un rey?
> Nisida: Si es tirano, poco importa.
>   Tu mal intento corrija
>   el cielo, pues tal ordena.[36]

The singer of text 67 suggests through the verbal maneuvers of the work that Pedro was the very epitome of the deficient and unsuitable king that the *Siete Partidas* sought to bar from authority. Beginning with line 33 of the text, the singer pursues a course in the *romance* which, although mindful of the theme of the first part of the narrative, is essentially an evaluation of Pedro's unsuitable behavior. The evaluation is carried out as follows:

First, the singer introduces the King's mistress, María de Padilla, into the work. This woman, who was such a powerful influence on Pedro that he allowed himself to become involved in the most contemptible of predicaments at her suggestion (seen in lines 42a-69b), is characterized in a double attributive as "aquella falsa traidora" (34a). She is made by the singer to write a letter to the King in which she (presumably) advises him of the information given in the opening lines of the text. Her letter provides a kind of negative guidance to the audience—of the same nature as the words spoken by Moraima in the *romance* discussed in section 3C of this study. Comparators (principally, negative clauses) are used throughout to pointedly defeat any expectations the audience might have had with respect to the character of the woman whose words so influenced the King. The singer begins by negating the reasonings of María's letter, stating, "No estaba bien informada" (35a), then proceeds to highlight her evil character, couching the clauses of the letter in negative constructions. This evaluative device, similar to the rhetorical trope *litotes*, or understatement by denial of the opposite, repeatedly suggests to the listeners the treachery of the King's closest counselor. María says, for example, "que no te hice traición   ni consentir la quería" (37a-37b). The idea that María is in fact a *falsa traidora* is underscored in this line by the very presumptions her words try to refute. It should also be mentioned that the opening line of María's letter, "Yo, tu leal servidora,   doña María de Padilla" (36a-36b), lends itself particularly well to the possibility of the use of intonation by the singer to indicate sarcasm. This would complement the ironic note of the mistress's own words, encouraging the audience to take a negative attitude towards María and her letter.

The singer's evaluation of María finds its natural sequel in the evaluation of Pedro which follows. Pedro has, of course, already been negatively evaluated through the characterization of his mistress. But in the remaining lines of the narrative, the King is not only shown as immoral in his relationship with María, but also, in his behavior as king. This is the second step in the singer's evaluation of Pedro as a king whose actions were in nearly every respect contrary to those expected of a monarch.

The *Siete Partidas* made quite clear the type of character required for the suitable fulfillment of kingly duties. For one, a king was expected to be equal in all ways to the exalted office he held. This meant temperance, self-control, good judgement, and a recognition of duty on the part of the monarch.[37] Text 67 dramatizes, through an alternation of standard narrative tenses and present, imperfect, and progressive clauses, the notion that these qualities were all lacking in Pedro. First of all, Pedro was so influenced by the evil María de Padilla that he was unable to accurately judge the advice she gave to him. The text shows the King gathering together all of his best people in Tarifa, rashly abandoning his official duties to pursue the bad information of *aquella falsa traidora* (42a-50b). The singer then focuses in on the unfortunate results of this foolish action. In a narrative digression which ultimately plays an evaluative role, the story is told of the King who is ignominiously wounded by his own palace guards. A weaving of imperfect and preterite clauses sets the scene in motion ("el rey tomaba la vía" [51b], "las puertas halló cerradas" [54a], "que cabe el muro yacía" [55b], etc.), while a series of present tense clauses actualizes the disgrace ("las guardas están velando" [60a], "muy muchas piedras le tiran" [60b]).

The dramatization of the scene emphatically raises the issue of Pedro's lack of self-control (he impetuously knocks on the palace doors "como si fuera de día" [59b]), and it ironically suggests Pedro's estrangement from his own home and people (e.g., the imperfect clause, "donde posarse solía" [58b], and the direct discourse passage in which García López Osorio must convince the King's own guards of his identity [63a-63b]). More importantly, however, the digression points to the general notion that Pedro's behavior violated the principles upon which a king should form himself. As the laws of the *Siete Partidas* show, the Castilians held clear standards of kingly duties and behavior. The responsibility of the people to remind the king of his deficiencies and to recall him to his duties was also clear. The singer uses these audience attitudes within the text of the *romance* to create a situation in which Pedro's inadequate behavior is dramatized. As a consequence, the audience is encouraged to connect Pedro's inappropriate behavior with his actual overthrow, which was known to them outside the *romance*. In this fashion, the singer sought to legitimize the Trastámaras.

The *romance* ends in a Coda (66a-69b) which brings the story up-to-date and terminates its action. The Resolution, as the audience well knew, was the murder of Fadrique by Pedro—an injustice which further contributed to the foundation of the Trastámaran takeover.

Text 67 is a very interesting text in that, while the singer seems to call upon the audience to treat the *romance* as a single narrative, there is clearly a division in the work which results in the assumption of two somewhat different evaluative postures. The first part of the *romance,* through the perpetuation of a text hostile to Blanca and Fadrique, establishes "pure" and royal descent for the Almirante de Castilla family. The second part asserts legitimacy for the Trastámaran usurpation. There is, however, a unifying principle to the text. This is the person of María de Padilla, whose mention in line 33 provides a link between the two divisions. It was a matter of historical record that María was a great friend of the Jews, and Pedro was often accused of compassion for this group because of his mistress's influence.[38] In combining the claim of *pureza de sangre* with that of legitimacy through the introduction of María de Padilla into the text, the pro-Trastámaran singer converted the insinuation of Jewish blood in the Almirante de Castilla family tree into a suggestion of impropriety in Pedro's own house. The narrative thus functions as a unit, single-mindedly impugning the deposed legal heir to the Castilian throne.

3. The *Romance del rey don Pedro*

The *romance* versions discussed above point to the *Romancero* as an ideal vehicle for evaluation. The *Romancero,* a tradition "que vive en variantes," allows one singer to use a predecessor's material in a totally unexpected way. Thus, in the previous versions, the accusation of adultery between Pedro's queen and his half brother, condemnatory and scandalous in one oral literary setting, became the basis of a claim to royalty and a refutation of "unclean" blood in another.

The following texts similarly show modifications in the evaluative strategies of different *romance* versions as resulting from the reworking of texts within different oral literary situations.

The two versions of the *Romance del rey don Pedro* to be discussed in this section (cited in tables 4 and 5) both take an openly hostile view of the dethroned Castilian king. They tell the story of an otherworldly *pastor* who somehow finds his way to the field in which the King is hunting. He accuses the King of murdering his brother, exiling his mother, and imprisoning his wife. He foresees doom for Pedro if he does not return to Blanca, and, in one version, slanders the King's daughters and prophesies succession by Enrique de Trastámara, Pedro's half brother.[39] Finally, the *pastor* disappears—as mysteriously as he had earlier arrived.

The *Romance del rey don Pedro* texts are *romances noticieros* in the sense that their purpose was to report the details of a newsworthy event. But the way in which each version carries out this function demonstrates that the texts served the vital interests of their propagator's political allegiance.

Text 66a, the first version to be studied here (see table 4), is a text which responds to the conflicts of the post-Pedro years with insinuations that not only Pedro but his descendants as well were unsuitable for leadership in Castile. It further suggests that the insinuations it makes are reflective of divine prophecy and God's will. This was essential, as will later be shown, for characteristic of Castilian thinking on kingship at that time was the concept of divinely inspired and sanctioned rule.

The conflicts upon which the story in the *romance* is founded are those that surrounded Enrique de Trastámara as he attempted to establish Trastámaran rule and resolve the bitter strife which marked his takeover. One of the most difficult problems Enrique faced in this respect was the so-called Atlantic question discussed by Luis Suárez Fernández. For mercantile reasons, supremacy for Castile in the Atlantic Ocean had long been considered a necessity. The Castilians needed to maintain trade routes for wool, iron, and wine from the Cantabrian ports to Flanders. But the Portuguese, to whose service many of Pedro's supporters had gone, threatened Trastámaran Castile's security in the Atlantic.[40] In 1371, Castile signed a peace treaty with Portugal, but the battle of the Atlantic was far from over. As Suárez Fernández comments:

> It was just at that point that the fiercest enemy the Trastámara's were to have during the next fifteen years appeared on the scene: John of Gaunt, duke of Lancaster, who married Peter I's daughter Constance in Roquefort (September, 1371) and assumed the title of King of Castile. ("The Atlantic" 60)

The objective of Pedro's descendants was clear: they sought to break the strength of Trastámaran rule by gaining control of the trade routes, using the Atlantic question as an opening for their own return to power.

TABLE 4

Evaluative Clauses in the *Romance del rey don Pedro el Cruel* (Text 66a)

	a	b
1	Por los campos de Jerez	a caza va el rey don Pedro
2	en llegando a una laguna,	allí quiso ver un vuelo.
3	Vido volar una garza,	desparóle un sacre nuevo,
4	remontárale un neblí,	a sus pies cayera muerto.
5	A sus pies cayó el neblí,	túvolo por mal agüero.
6	Tanto volaba la garza,	parece llegar al cielo.
7	Por donde la garza sube	vio bajar un bulto negro;
8	mientras más se acerca el bulto,	más temor le va poniendo
9	con el abajarse tanto,	parece llegar al suelo
10	delante de su caballo	a cinco pasos de trecho:
11	dél salió un pastorcico,	sale llorando y gimiendo,
12	la cabeza desgreñada,	revuelto trae el cabello,
13	con los pies llenos de abrojos	y el cuerpo lleno de vello;
14	en su mano una culebra	y en la otra un puñal sangriento
15	en el hombro una mortaja,	una calavera al cuello;
16	a su lado de trailla	traía un perro negro;
17	los aullidos que daba	a todos ponían gran miedo,
18	y a grandes voces decía:	Morirás, el rey don Pedro,
19	que mataste sin justicia	los mejores de tu reino:
20	mataste tu propio hermano	el Maestre, sin consejo,
21	y desterraste a tu madre:	a Dios darás cuenta de ello.
22	Tienes presa a doña Blanca,	enojaste a Dios por ello,
23	que si tornas a quererla	darte ha Dios un heredero,
24	y si no, por cierto sepas	te vendrá desmán por ello;
25	serán malas las tus hijas	por tu culpa y mal gobierno,
26	y tu hermano don Henrique	te habrá de heredar el reino:
27	morirás a puñaladas:	tu casa será el infierno.—
28	Todo esto recontado,	desapareció el bulto negro.

Source for text 66a: Menéndez y Pelayo, *Antología de poetas líricos castellanos* 8: 128-29.

Continued on next page

Table 4—*Continued*

Comparators	Correlatives	Explicatives
Negative Clauses:	**Present Tense Clauses:**	5b túvolo por mal agüero
19a *que mataste sin justicia*	1b a caza va el rey don	9a con el abajarse tanto
20b *el Maestre, sin consejo*	Pedro	25b *por tu culpa y mal*
	6b parece llegar al cielo	*gobierno*
Future Clauses:	7a Por donde la garza sube	
18b *Morirás, el rey don*	9b parece llegar al suelo	
Pedro	12b revuelto trae el cabello	
21b *a Dios darás cuenta de*		
ello	**Imperfect Clauses:**	
25a *serán malas las tus hijas*	6a Tanto volaba la garza	
26b *te habrá de heredar el*	16b traía un perro negro	
reino	17a- los aullidos que daba	
27a- *morirás a puñaladas*	17b a todos ponían gran	
27b *tu casa será el infierno*	miedo	
	18a y a grandes voces decía	
Si **Clauses:**		
23a- *que si tornas a quererla*	**Progessive Clauses:**	
23b *darte ha Dios un*	8b más temor le va	
heredero	poniendo	
24a- *y si no, por cierto sepas*	11b sale llorando y gimiendo	
24b *te vendrá desmán por*		
ello	**Attributives:**	
	13a- con los pies llenos de	
	abrojos	
	13b y el cuerpo lleno de	
	vello	
	20a- *mataste tu propio*	
	hermano	
	20b *el Maestre, sin consejo*	

Note: clauses contained within direct discourse passages are in italics.

Doña Constanza, Pedro's daughter and the wife of the Duke of Lancaster who proclaimed himself King of Castile, was no doubt the target of the slander against Pedro's daughters found in the *romance*—"y serán malas las tus hijas" (25a). She also represents the *infierno* which the *pastor* prophesied Pedro's house would become as a result of his behavior during his rule (27b). But the fact that the slander and the prediction were claimed as divinely ordained gives the clearest indication that the singer of the text intended to insist on the legitimacy of the Trastámaran succession to the Castilian throne through the course of the *romance*. This was certainly the evaluative purpose of the composition.

The *romance* consists of an Orientation section (1a-2b), a Complicating Action section (3a-11a), an Evaluation section (11b-26b), a Resolution (27a-27b), and a Coda (28). The point of the *romance*'s narrative is, as will be seen, to evaluate the Complicating Action of the work in a manner which impugned not only Pedro, but his descendants as well. For the evaluative devices which complement this endeavor, see table 4.

The *romance* begins as the singer positions the audience within the action of the text—"a caza va el rey don Pedro / en llegando a una laguna" (1b-2a)—using present and progressive clauses. It continues in traditional narrative form, with a majority of preterite constructions in the Complicating Action section. At key moments, the singer interjects present, progressive, or imperfect clauses, building suspense for subsequent actions and events (e.g., 6a, 6b, 7a, 8a, 8b, and 9b). In 11b, the events of the Complicating Action are evaluated. In a manner that emphasizes both the tellability of the narrative and the attitudes that the audience ought to take with respect to the unusual circumstances of the Complicating Action, the listeners are guided through the text as the singer defines for them the precise nature of the activities described in the work.

The first lines of the Evaluation consist of present tense clauses (e.g., *sale* [11b], *trae* [12b]). In the lines that follow, however, verbal constructions—those dynamic expressions of action that are characteristically the mainstay of the *Romancero*[41]—give way to a predominance of adjectives and adjectival phrases. These clauses appear in the evaluation chart as a series of correlatives. It is interesting to note that the descriptive expressions used to evaluate the action of the *romance* are presented in sequence, without benefit of verbal connection. This introduces an unexpected complexity into the *romance* which functions to rivet the audience's attention on the portrayal of its principal character. In effect, this description says to the audience that the *pastor* of the *romance* was no ordinary shepherd, moralizing in a conventional manner. This *pastor* was divine and his words should be seriously heeded.

The dramatic presentation of the shepherd who prophesies Pedro's doom points to the dynamic which makes the story tellable within the oral literary situation of the post-Pedro years. Responding to the tenor of the times, in which Pedro's descendants sought to re-establish their authority in Castilian affairs, it draws attention to the "fact" that the outcome of Pedro's reign— i.e., the Trastámaran takeover—was a predetermined consequence of his unjust rule.

The audience, psychologically prepared for the shepherd's speech through the suspense generated by the string of attributives in the first lines of the Evaluation, listens intently as the supernatural creature speaks. This suspense, which is further enhanced by the three imperfect clauses (17a, 17b, 18a) that precede the *pastor*'s soliloquy, calls attention to the importance of the prophecy.

The first clause uttered by the otherworldly shepherd functions as a comparator. "Morirás, el rey don Pedro" (18b), he cries, alluding to the outcome of Pedro's fratricidal struggle with Enrique. He then rehearses for the audience a list of some of Pedro's most serious misdeeds: Pedro killed unjustly the best people in his kingdom (19a-19b), he killed his own brother (20a-20b), he exiled his mother (21a-21b), and he imprisoned his wife (22a-22b).

As in the earlier discussion of the *Romance de doña Blanca,* it is instructive to view the evaluative content of text 66a within the context of the attitudes and beliefs held by its audience. These attitudes and beliefs may be in some way understood by examining both the officially sanctioned and customary codes of the Castilian populace. The *Siete Partidas* may once again be useful as an example. These codes make particularly clear the principles to which a king was expected to adhere. The very first principle was that the king must know, love, and fear God, for the aid of God is necessary to govern in justice and right reason.[42] The predictions made by the *pastorico profeta* in the *romance* evidence the failure of Pedro to look to God for aid in his rule. In a series of future (21b), present (22a), preterite (19a, 20a, 21a), and *si* (23a-25b) clauses, the singer weaves prophecies for the future with details of the past in an ultimate demonstration of Pedro as a king formed not on the love and fear of God, but rather, on ambition, vice, and cruelty—characteristics specifically warned against in the Castilian legal codes.[43] The *pastor* is God's messenger, and he speaks from the standpoint of one who knows intimately God's law. Pedro, he says, has broken that law ("enojaste a Dios . . ." [22b]) and will have to pay a price for it ("a Dios darás cuenta de ello" [21b]). The nature of Pedro's punishment is suggested in the series of future clauses which reminds the audience of the contemporary circumstances of conflict between Pedro's descendants and the Trastámaras, and an explicative which specifically shows the listeners that the King's descendants are invested with the shortcomings of their father ("serán malas las tus hijas   por tu culpa y mal gobierno" [25a-25b]).

The audience, which perhaps brought to the oral literary situation a mixture of political sentiments, would have been impressed by the rich description of the scene in which the *pastor* confronts King Pedro. This scene, moreover, might have encouraged them to take the *pastor*'s prediction as a warning to the Castilian people. After all, two of the shepherd's prophecies had already come true: Pedro died violently and was succeeded by his brother Enrique. That his daughter was doomed bore negatively on the support she and her husband might expect from the Castilians. The singer thus subtly maneuvers the listener from the description of past events to that of the present. The *romance*, sung within the context of Enrique de Trastámara's antagonism towards Pedro's descendants, becomes a vehicle not for pious moralizing, but for the evaluation of a real political problem.

Text 66 bears many resemblances to 66a. Its evaluative purpose is similar to that of the former text: it seeks to discredit King Pedro's camp. Like text 66a, this *romance* must have been composed after the Castilian king's demise, for it provides an accurate description of events that followed Pedro's downfall. There are, however, a few subtle differences between the two *romances* which mark a distinction between their respective evaluative stances. Text 66 and its evaluation chart appear in table 5.

Text 66 begins with an Orientation section like that of 66a. The location is Jerez (1a); the situation, *la caza* (1b); the character, *el rey don Pedro* (1b). After the Orientation, the Complicating Action section of the *romance* provides a basic answer to the question of what happened during the events of the *romance*. Six and one-half lines of principally narrative (i.e., temporally ordered) clauses recapitulate the action (3a-9a). Finally, a change of aspect in 9b ("llorando viene y gimiendo") marks the opening of the Evaluation section. This also is structured in a manner similar to text 66a, with an interruption in the narrative sequence which allows a description of the *pastor* and a direct quotation of his words.

The description in text 66, although somewhat different from that in 66a, creates a comparably frightening impression. There is a long series of attributives (12a-13b), and the terrifying impression made by the otherworldly creature is heightened and lengthened by them. Furthermore, the description is made increasingly vivid through an imperfect clause, "aullidos daba muy tristes" (13a), which produces the sensation of actual, ongoing "wailing," and the use of the present progressive (e.g., "sus cabellos va mesando   la su cara va rompiendo" [14a-14b]), which brings a vital spark to the *pastor*'s characterization.

The principal distinction between texts 66a and 66, however, lies in the fact that the latter text specifically evaluates Pedro in terms of the politically charged Spanish frontier (hence its mention of Jerez [1a] and Medina Sidonia [7a]), while the former is concerned with the interests of Pedro's descendants in regaining power.

The different evaluative posture of text 66 is made clear, interestingly, in orienting material. This material is placed not only at the beginning of the narrative, but also at strategic points later on in the text. Thus in the Complicating Action section, one finds information which is at once orienting and evaluative.[44]

The *romance,* it may be recalled, began with a citation of location for the events reported in the narrative: "los campos de Jerez" (1a). There is nothing unusual about this particular setting for the action of the text in that "the energies of Spain at this epoch were concentrated at Sevilla"[45] and Pedro preferred to reside in the South. It is perfectly logical, therefore, that the King should be hunting "por los campos de Jerez," as he is in both texts 66a and 66. That the *bulto negro* (7b) concealing the prophetic shepherd should appear from Medina Sidonia in text 66 is, on the other hand, more significant. Medina Sidonia is a marked lexical item within the context of anti-Pedro ballads, for it was part of the Trastámaran stronghold in southwestern Andalusia. As MacKay points out:[46]

unlike their half-brother King Pedro, the Trastamaran bastards were the children of Leonor de Guzmán and were consequently connected with the two most powerful lineages of south-western Andalusia, the Ponce de León and Guzmanes. (28)

The fact that the *bulto*'s origin is specified in the text as the *patria* of the Trastámaras indicates that it is a purposefully intended reminder to the listeners that Enrique de Trastámara was a Guzmán. It is fitting that the threat to King Pedro should have come from Medina Sidonia, for indeed it was from this territory that his conqueror did ultimately arrive. In effect, the use of orienting material in the Complicating Action section of the *romance* serves an eminently evaluative purpose. It equates Trastámaran interests with divine interests, translating the shepherd's warning to the King into a kind of divine sanction for the eventual overthrow of Pedro and the Trastámaran takeover.

The evaluative use of orienting material is again evident in the opening line of the *pastor*'s speech. The shepherd's first words, a repetition— "Castilla, Castilla, . . ." (16a-16b)—emphatically locate the seat of the monarchy as a doomed territory. Castilla was, as MacKay comments, "a vague area 'out there' and can be contrasted with specific locations [in the ballads] such as . . . Medina Sidonia" (18). The late Castilian kings from this vague "out there" had defaulted on the so-called manifest destiny of the Reconquest (MacKay 19), and their remoteness from the lesser lords of the frontier is evident in many *fronterizo* ballads which are far more concerned with the exploits of local leaders than with kings and great nobles. The singer in text 66 is clearly addressing a southern audience. He uses such localizations (discussed earlier) to strike a note of familiarity and nationalistic sympathy in the minds of the audience. The prophecy of doom, on the other

TABLE 5

Evaluative Clauses in the *Romance del rey don Pedro* (Text 66)

	a	b
1	Por los campos de Jerez	a caza va el rey don Pedro;
2	allegóse a una laguna,	allí quiso ver un vuelo.
3	Vio salir de ella una garza,	remontóle un sacre nuevo;
4	echóle un neblí preciado,	degollado se le ha luego;
5	a sus pies cayó el neblí,	túvolo por mal agüero.
6	Sube la garza muy alta,	parece entrar en el cielo.
7	De hacia Medina Sidonia	vio venir un bulto negro:
8	cuanto más se le allegaba,	poniéndole va más miedo.
9	Salió dél un pastorcico,	llorando viene y gimiendo,
10	con un bastón en sus manos,	los ojos en tierra puestos,
11	sin bonete su cabeza,	todo vestido de duelo,
12	descalzo, lleno de espinas.	De trailla trae un perro,
13	aullidos daba muy tristes,	concertados con su duelo;
14	sus cabellos va mesando,	la su cara va rompiendo;
15	el duelo hace tan triste,	que al rey hace poner miedo.
16	A voces dice:—Castilla,	Castilla, perderte has cedo,
17	que en ti se verte la sangre	de tus nobles caballeros;
18	mátaslos contra justicia,	reclaman a Dios del cielo.—
19	Los gritos daba muy altos,	todos se espantan de vello.
20	Su cara lleva de sangre;	allegóse al rey don Pedro;
21	dijo:—Rey, lo que te digo,	sin duda te verná presto:
22	serás muy acalumniado,	y serás por armas muerto.
23	Quieres mal a doña Blanca,	a Dios ensañas por ello;
24	perderás por ello el reino.	Si quieres volver con ella,
25	darte ha Dios un heredero.	El rey fue mucho turbado,
26	mandó el pastor fuese preso;	mandó hacer gran pesquisa
27	si la reina fuera en esto.	El pastor se les soltara,
28	nadie sabe qué se ha hecho.	Mandó matar a la reina
29	ese día a un caballero,	pareciéndole acababa
30	con su muerte el mal agüero.	

Source for text 66: Menéndez y Pelayo, *Antología de poetas líricos castellanos* 8: 126-27.

Continued on next page

Table 5—*Continued*

Comparators	Correlatives	Explicatives
Negative Clauses:	**Present Perfect Clauses:**	5b túvolo por mal agüero
11a sin bonete su cabeza	4b degollado se le ha luego	17a- *que en ti se verte la*
21b *sin duda te verná presto*	16b *Castilla, perderte has*	*sangre*
28a nadie sabe qué se ha	*cedo*	17b *de tus nobles caballeros*
hecho	28a nadie sabe qué se ha	
	hecho	
Future Clauses:		
21b *sin duda te verná presto*	**Present Tense Clauses:**	
22a- *serás muy acalumniado*	1b a caza va el rey don	
22b *y serás por armas muerto*	Pedro	
24a *perderás por ello el*	6a- Sube la garza muy alta	
reino	6b parece entrar en el cielo	
	12b De trailla trae un perro	
Si **Clauses:**	15a el duelo hace tan triste	
24b *Si quieres volver con ella*	16a A voces dice: —*Castilla*	
25a *darte ha Dios un*	18a- *mátaslos contra justicia*	
heredero	18b *reclaman a Dios del cielo*	
	19b todos se espantan de	
Subjunctive Clauses:	vello	
26a mandó el pastor fuese	20a Su cara lleva de sangre	
preso	21a *Rey, lo que te digo*	
	23a *Quieres mal a doña*	
	Blanca	
	28a nadie sabe qué se ha	
	hecho	
	Imperfect Clauses:	
	8a cuanto más se le allegaba	
	13a aullidos daba muy tristes	
	19a Los gritos daba muy	
	altos	
	29b pareciéndole acababa	
	Progressive Clauses:	
	8b poniéndole va más	
	miedo	
	9b llorando viene y	
	gimiendo	
	14a- sus cabellos va mesando	
	14b la su cara va rompiendo	
	Appositives:	
	12a descalzo, lleno de	
	espinas	
	13a- aullidos daba muy tristes	
	13b concertados con su	
	duelo	

Note: clauses contained within direct discourse passages are in italics.

hand, is addressed to distant Castile, where noble blood has been shed by a king whose lineage is derived far from the *campos* in which he finds himself in his encounter with the shepherd.

The remainder of text 66 complements the evaluative stance established through the strategically placed orienting material. The *pastor*'s speech continues with a series of future tense forms (21b-22b) suggesting events that are as yet unrealized within the text but that the audience knew to have actually occurred. Pedro's loss of the throne was not only justified, the *romance* indicates, but also fated. And if the mention of unwarranted slaughter of Castilian nobility in 17b were not enough justification for the Trastámaran takeover, doña Blanca, the sure symbol of Pedro's cruelty, is introduced. The *pastor* states that if Pedro returns to his queen, he will have *un heredero* (25a). If not, he will lose his kingdom.

Every line and every element of the *pastor*'s speech builds towards the final prophecy of the *romance*: King Pedro will be dethroned ("perderás el reino" [24a]). This part of the Evaluation section is presented almost entirely in terms of certain events and actions that will happen if others do not. The singer thus secures the listeners' sympathy for the anti-Pedro side. After all, the Castilian king had been forewarned by a prophetic shepherd from the very land of his enemies. The King chose not to heed the words of the otherworldly creature. Instead, as the Resolution shows, he imprisoned the *pastor* and had the Queen murdered. These rash actions, the audience knew, sealed his doom. The Coda of the *romance* can only be ironic: "pareciéndole acababa / con su [la de doña Blanca] muerte el mal agüero" (29b-30a). The death of doña Blanca, this Coda says, by no means nullified the *pastor*'s predictions. Rather, it was just another detail in the eventual demise of King Pedro. Unmindful of a king's duties towards his wife, his family, and his parents (also specified in the *Siete Partidas*[47]), Pedro ultimately justified his own overthrow by the Trastámarans.

4. The *Romance de la muerte de la reina Blanca*

The *Romance del rey don Pedro* versions (particularly text 66) complement other *romances* which take up specifically the subject of Queen Blanca's death as a rallying point for the anti-Pedro forces. However, whereas the *Romance del rey don Pedro* suggested that the King's dealings with his wife were but one element in a long list of deficiencies, these other *romances* single out Pedro's treatment of Blanca as the dominant factor in his ultimate demise.

Two versions of the *Romance de la muerte de la reina Blanca* are instances of texts in which Blanca's death is shown as an overriding concern of those who sought to overthrow the King. These *romances* seem to have been composed by Pedro's enemies during the years of strife between the King and pro-Trastámaran forces, for they evaluate with a sense of urgency a situation which occurred some years before the Trastámaran victory (Blanca died in 1361; Enrique de Trastámara came to power in 1369). The texts and their rendering into the proposed syntactic categories appear in tables 6 and 7. Text 68 (see table 6), the first *romance* to be considered here, presupposes, like the other texts examined in this chapter, certain shared information between the singer and the audience. The *romance* begins with a kind of Abstract (1a-6b) which builds on the audience's foreknowledge of the situation in which King Pedro abandoned his wife for his mistress immediately following their wedding ceremony.

The Abstract is presented first through an evaluation by King Pedro of his actions towards his mistress and his wife. In rapid succession there are two negatives, one imperative, one conditional, and a long (2b-3b) explicative clause. The explicative presents Pedro's explanation for his unions with both María de Padilla and doña Blanca; it is stated in terms of affection for the former ("por vuestro amor" [2b]) and disdain for the latter ("por hacer menosprecio" [3a]). The conditional statement preceding the explicative is the motivation for the explanation. It introduces the possibility of the King's wrongdoing ("si me descasé dos veces" [2a]) and makes way for the rationalization which follows. The three comparators in the second line of the text evaluate an unseen state of affairs; that is to say, the circumstances of the mistress, who presumably feels a certain jealously towards the legal wife of the King. Pedro, presupposing this envy, demands that María end her unhappiness, for, as he goes on to explain, all has been done for her benefit.

These first lines of the *romance* quite clearly go beyond basic narrative sequence. They deal with a situation that is not defined in the narrative yet which is, as has already been briefly mentioned, part of the cognitive background of the audience. In this same vein, the text continues with two and one-half lines (4a-6a) that diverge from the usual forthrightness of the *Romancero* art in their use of a metaphor to enhance the vividness of the narrative which follows. The King, who continues as the speaker in these lines, says he has sent to Medina Sidonia for *un pendón*—"será de color de sangre, de lágrimas su labor" (5a-5b). The *pendón de sangre* refers to the corpse of doña Blanca who, as the Complicating Action shows, was ordered cruelly murdered on her husband's prescription. The metaphorical relation the *pendón* bears to the Queen is made explicit through the location of Medina Sidonia where, as tradition has it, the Queen was imprisoned, as well as through the description of the *pendón* as bloody and tearful.

Like the other Abstracts considered in this study, lines 1a-6b encapsulate the story contained in the narrative. In brief, they report the King's dispatch of murderers to Medina Sidonia to do away with the Queen. However, the employment of a trope to accomplish its end marks this Abstract as highly evaluative in and of itself. The total impact of the image of a dead and bloodstained doña Blanca carried as a standard by the King of Castile cannot be

TABLE 6

Evaluative Clauses in the *Romance de doña Blanca de Borbón* (Text 68)

	a	b
1	Doña María de Padilla,	no os mostredes triste, no;
2	si me descasé dos veces,	hícelo por vuestro amor,
3	y por hacer menosprecio	de doña Blanca de Borbón:
4	a Medina Sidonia envío	que me labren un pendón;
5	será de color de sangre	de lágrimas su labor:
6	tal pendón, doña María,	se hace por vuestro amor.—
7	Llamara Alonso Ortiz,	que es un honrado varón,
8	para que fuese a Medina	a dar fin a la labor.
9	Respondió Alonso Ortiz;	Eso, señor, no haré yo,
10	que quien mata a su señora	es aleve a su señor.—
11	El rey no le respondiera;	en su cámara se entró:
12	enviara por dos maceros,	los cuales él escogió.
13	Estos fueron a la reina,	halláronla en oración;
14	la reina como los viera,	casi muerta se cayó;
15	mas después que en sí tornara,	esforzada les habló:
16	—Ya sé a qué venís, amigos,	que mi alma lo sintió;
17	aqueso que está ordenado	no se puede excusar, no.
18	¡Oh Castilla! ¿Qué te hice?	No por cierto traición.
19	¡Oh Francia, mi dulce tierra!	¡Oh mi casa de Borbón!
20	Hoy cumplo dieciséis años,	a los diecisiete muero yo.
21	El rey no me ha conocido,	con las vírgenes me vo.
22	Doña María de Padilla,	esto te pardono yo;
23	por quitarte de cuidado	lo hace el rey mi señor.—
24	Los maceros le dan priesa,	ella pide confesión;
25	perdonáralos a ellos,	y puesta en su oración,
26	danle golpes con las mazas,	y ansí la triste murió.

Source for text 68: Menéndez y Pelayo, *Antología de poetas líricos castellanos* 8: 134-35.

Continued on next page

Table 6—*Continued*

Comparators	Correlatives	Explicatives
Negative Clauses:	**Present Perfect Clauses:**	2b *hícelo por vuestro amor*
1b *no os mostredes triste, no*	21a *El rey no me ha conocido*	3a- *y por hacer menosprecio*
11a El rey no le respondiera		3b *de doña Blanca de*
17b *no se puede excusar, no*	**Present Tense Clauses:**	*Borbón*
18b *No por cierto traición*	4a *a Medina Sidonia envío*	4b *que me labren un*
21a *El rey no me ha conocido*	16a *Ya sé a qué venís,*	*pendón*
	amigos	6b *se hace por vuestro amor*
Future Tense Clauses:	17a *aqueso que está*	7b *que es un honrado varón*
5a *será de color de sangre*	*ordenado*	10a- *que quien mata a su*
9b *Eso, señor, no haré yo*	20a- *Hoy cumplo dieciséis*	*señora*
	años	10b *es aleve a su señor*
Si Clauses:	20b *a los diecisiete muero yo*	16b *que mi alma lo sintió*
2a- *si me descasé dos veces*	21b *con las vírgenes me vo*	23a- *por quitarte de cuidado*
2b *hícelo por vuestro amor*	22b *esto te pardono yo*	23b *lo hace el rey mi señor*
	?4a- Los maceros le dan	
Subjunctive Clauses:	priesa	
7a Llamara Alonso Ortiz	24b ella pide confesión	
8a para que fuese a Medina	26a danle golpes con las	
	mazas	
Imperative Clauses:		
1b *no os mostredes triste, no*	**Attributives:**	
	19a- *¡Oh Francia, mi dulce*	
Interrogative Clauses:	*tierra!*	
18a *¡Oh Castilla! ¿Qué te*	19b *¡Oh mi casa de Borbón!*	
hice?		

Note: clauses contained within direct discourse passages are in italics.

TABLE 7

Evaluative Clauses in the *Romance de la muerte de la reina Blanca* (Text 68a)

	a	b
1	Doña María de Padilla,	no os mostráis triste vos,
2	que si me casé dos veces,	hícelo por vuestra pro,
3	y por hacer menosprecio	a doña Blanca de Borbón.
4	A Medina Sidonia envío	a que me labre un pendón:
5	será el color de su sangre,	de lágrimas la labor.
6	Tal pendón, doña María,	le haré hacer por vos.
7	Y llamara a Iñigo Ortiz,	un excelente varón:
8	díjole fuese a Medina	a dar fin a tal labor.
9	Respondiera Iñigo Ortiz:	—Aqueso no faré yo,
10	que quien mata a su señora	hace aleve a su señor.—
11	El rey, de aquesto enojado,	a su cámara se entró,
12	y a un ballestero de maza	el rey entregar mandó.
13	Aqueste vino a la reina	y hallóla en oración.
14	Cuando vido al ballestero,	la su triste muerte vio.
15	Aquél le dijo:—Señora,	el rey acá me envió
16	a que ordenéis vuestra alma	con aquél que la crio,
17	que vuestra hora es llegada,	no puedo alargalla yo.
18	—Amigo, dijo la reina,	mi muerte os perdono yo;
19	si el rey mi señor lo manda,	hágase lo que ordenó.
20	Confesión no se me niegue,	sino pido a Dios perdón.—
21	Sus lágrimas y gemidos	al macero enterneció;
22	con la voz flaca, temblando,	esto a decir comenzó:
23	— ¡Oh Francia, mi noble tierra!	¡Oh mi sangre de Borbón!
24	Hoy cumplo decisiete años,	en los deciocho voy:
25	el rey no me ha conocido,	con las vírgenes me voy.
26	Castilla, di ¿qué te hice?	No te hice traición.
27	Las coronas que me diste	de sangre y sospiros son;
28	mas otra terné en el cielo	que será de más valor.—
29	Y dichas estas palabras,	el macero la hirió:
30	los sesos de su cabeza	por la sala los sembró.

Source for text 68a: Menéndez y Pelayo, *Antología de poetas líricos castellanos* 8: 135-36.

Continued on next page

Table 7—*Continued*

Comparators	Correlatives	Explicatives
Negative Clauses:	**Present Perfect Clauses:**	2b *hícelo por vuestra pro*
1b *no os mostráis triste vos*	25a *el rey no me ha conocido*	3a- *y por hacer menosprecio*
9b *Aqueso no faré yo*		3b *a doña Blanca de*
17b *no puedo alargalla yo*	**Present Tense Clauses:**	*Borbón*
20a- *Confesión no se me*	17b *no puedo alargalla yo*	4b *a que me labre un*
niegue	18b *mi muerte os perdono yo*	*pendón*
20b *sino pido a Dios perdón*	20b *sino pido a Dios perdón*	6b *le haré hacer por vos*
25a *el rey no me ha conocido*	24a- *Hoy cumplo decisiete*	7b *un excelente varón*
26b *No te hice traición*	*años*	8b *a dar fin a tal labor*
	24b *en los deciocho voy*	10a- *que quien mata a su*
Future Tense Clauses:	25b *con las vírgenes me voy*	*señora*
5a *será el color de su*		10b *hace aleve a su señor*
sangre	**Attributives:**	17a *que vuestra hora es*
9b *Aqueso no faré yo*	23a- *¡Oh Francia, mi noble*	*llegada*
28a- *mas otra terné en el cielo*	*tierra!*	
28b *que será de más valor*	23b *¡Oh mi sangre de*	
	Borbón!	
Si **Clauses:**		
2a- *que si me casé dos veces*	**Appositives:**	
2b *hícelo por vuestra pro*	22a con la voz flaca,	
19a *si el rey mi señor lo*	*temblando*	
manda		
Subjunctive Clauses:		
8a *díjole fuese a Medina*		
Imperative Clauses:		
16a *a que ordenéis vuestra*		
alma		
20a *Confesión no se me*		
niegue		
26a *Castilla, di*		
Interrogative Clauses:		
26a *¿qué te hice?*		

Note: clauses contained within direct discourse passages are in italics.

translated into logical terms. The emotional sensations the audience must feel at this metaphorical rendering of the story of the Queen's death goes beyond the intense feeling it will experience after the Queen's pathetic apostrophes later on in the work. The Abstract thus both summarizes and evaluates the narrative. It also, in its naming of doña María de Padilla, suggests, as Menéndez y Pelayo writes in *Tratado de los romances viejos,* her "complicidad, á lo menos moral, en este horrendo caso, que el rey ejecuta en obsequio y rendimiento amoroso por ella" (*Antología* 12: 133). The point of the *romance* is in this way made by the singer, who has King Pedro evaluate his own actions in this part of the text in such a manner as to precipitate the least sympathetic response in the audience for himself and his mistress.

Lines 7a through 15b constitute the Complicating Action section of the *romance.* They consist of seven and one-half lines of straight narrative (7a-9a; 11a-15b) and one and one-half lines of direct discourse (9b-10b) by one Alonso Ortiz. These lines advance the plot of the *romance* with few interjections of evaluation. However, the direct discourse, which typically both continues and evaluates the Complicating Action, provides a kind of positive guidance to the audience. The *romance* encourages the listeners to be swayed by the speaker, Alonso Ortiz, by portraying him as *un honrado varón* (7b). It then shows how this honorable person was compelled to refuse to do the King's bidding in the horrible murder of Queen Blanca. Evaluating for the audience the King's disregard for the sacred bonds of matrimony in the murder he contemplates, Alonso Ortiz affirms in an explicative the oneness of a man with his wife. To kill the Queen would violate bonds of loyalty to the King, for ". . . quien mata a su señora   es aleve a su señor" (10a-10b). The Complicating Action ends with the touching narration of a pathetic scene: the Queen is found by her murderers in the midst of prayer. An eight-line Evaluation follows.

Lines 16a through 23b compose the main Evaluation section of the text. These lines form the soliloquy of doña Blanca. They contain three negatives (17b and 18b), one question (18a), six present tense forms (16a, 17a, 20, 21b, and 22b), one past participle (21a), and an explicative (23a-23b) which function, as Menéndez y Pelayo has commented in *Tratado,* to contrast "la resignación y piedad de la desvalida Reina con la barbarie de sus matadores" (*Antología* 12: 132). The singer has the Queen evaluate her impending doom through a series of four steps in which she first accepts her fate (16a-17b– Menéndez y Pelayo's "resignación"), then interrogates Castile (18a), exculpates herself from any wrongdoing (18b-21b), and finally, reintroduces the person of María de Padilla into the narrative through two lines in which she pronounces forgiveness for her rival (22a-23b).

These four steps correspond both semantically and syntactically to the singer's evaluative strategy in the *romance,* which is to discredit the King and his mistress and to sway public opinion against the monarch. The audience knows from the lines preceding the soliloquy that the Queen's words can be trusted. She is depicted as in the midst of prayer when the *maceros* enter her room. It is therefore the soulful outpourings of a pious woman that guide the listeners in their evaluation of the circumstances. Blanca successively negates the possibility of any rationalization for her murder ("no se puede excusar, no" [17b]); negates any suggestion of a crime she may have committed; contrasts Castile, which she holds responsible for her death, with France ("mi dulce tierra" [19a]) and the house of Bourbon; and explicates the crucial role of María de Padilla in her death. The soliloquy is in the expected present tense form, with the exception of 21a, which is marked by its departure from this tense. 21a makes use of a present perfect form in order to foreground the unsullied (and also pathetic, in that it demonstrates the Queen's prolonged deprivation of normal marital relations) past. The effect of the soliloquy is a devasting condemnation of the Castile of Pedro and his mistress.

The Evaluation section of the *romance* is followed by a two-line Resolution (24a-25b). In a final touch of pathos, the singer shows the Queen asking for confession, forgiving her own murderers, and, once again in the midst of prayer, being bludgeoned to death by the *maceros*. The present tense is heavily relied upon in the Resolution to display the dramatic intensity of the scene. The audience, which has been privy—as an audience—to the Queen's last words, now is positioned within the text itself in order to witness her cruel death. The Coda (26a) effectively closes the *romance*.

The *Romance de la reina Blanca* (text 68) must have been composed by *juglares* in the service of the Trastámaran faction, for it pronounces through its verses an effective and urgent call to all moral human beings to strive to topple the cruel Castilian king. Depicting Pedro as wickedly collaborating with his mistress in the heartless murder of Blanca, it equates the dead Queen with the monarchal standard. This sad story, developed through the lines of the text, lent the *romance* the makings of a highly transmittable tale. However, it also provided an artistic response to the Trastámaran policy decision to use the death of doña Blanca as a rallying point.

Of course it was by no means certain that Blanca died an unnatural death, and María's participation in her murder is even less likely. As Menéndez y Pelayo remarks:

A estas razones ya tan sensatas debe añadirse que los contemporáneos mismos dudaron del hecho, y admitieron la posibilidad de que la Reina hubiese sucumbido sin otro suplicio que el dolor y la tristeza de la cárcel, como se insinúa en un documento de origen francés, la primera vida anónima de Inocencio VI, inserta en la colección de Baluze. (*Antología* 12: 135)

But the impressive account given in the *romance* was perpetuated through the ballad tradition which preserved the story of a king who brutally murdered his wife for the sake of his mistress. This story, highly transmittable because of its universal human interest, quickly became the accepted version of Blanca's death. This is clear from the study of a text such as 67a (analyzed earlier) which, although favorable to the King, had to accept his involvement in Blanca's death as true. In fact, the *romance* version of the death of doña Blanca became the basis for the *Romance de doña Blanca* (text 67a) which sought to justify Pedro for his supposed part in the murder.

Text 68a (see table 7) is structured in roughly the same way as text 68. It contains a six-line Abstract (1a-6b), an eight-line Complicating Action section (7a-14b), a fourteen-line Evaluation (15a-28b), and a two-line Resolution (29a-30b). The principal difference between the two texts is that in text 68a, the singer expands the use of evaluative devices to include a dialogue between the Queen and her executioner (15a-20b), in which she manages to soften even the hardness of a *macero*'s heart (21); a speculation, in a present tense clause, by Blanca on her destiny in the afterlife (25b); and a more powerful choice of vocabulary in the description of the actual murder of the Queen. In these differences, text 68a manifests a greater force than text 68. It clearly presumes to identify Blanca as a saint and, consequently, the man responsible for her murder as a villain. The message of the *romance* is nowhere clearer than in the Queen's complaint against Castile: "Las coronas que me diste   de sangre y sospiros son" (27a-27b).

In the Evaluation section of the *romance* the Queen is once again the guiding voice. She does not initiate the dialogue—the *ballestero de maza* does—yet she shows the listeners, through her pious and merciful response to the murderer, her own virtuousness as opposed to the malevolence of those who seek to kill her. That this paragon of goodness and purity should meet such a dreadful end touches the *macero* who has been ordered to slay the Queen. He allows her to complete a long plaint, through which she alerts the audience to her moral rectitude ("el rey no me ha conocido   con las vírgenes me voy" [25a-25b]) and her nobility ("¡Oh Francia, mi noble tierra!   ¡Oh mi sangre de Borbón!" [23a-23b]), before carrying out the King's orders. In her final, heartrending line, doña Blanca predicts a blissful future for herself in heaven, further affirming her saintliness ("mas otra [corona] terné en el cielo   que será de más valor" [28a-28b]). She becomes, through the *romance,* a martyr for the Trastámaran side; a blood-stained banner which the King and his mistress will wear like an albatross until they are vanquished once and for all.

Text 68a, with its greater reliance on dialogue, shows particularly the fascinating interplay of linguistic structure and evaluation in the *Romancero.* Dialogue, or direct discourse, is a leading evaluative tool in the *romances,* for it enables the singer to dramatize and actualize the events of the narrative while directly involving the audience in the actions of the text through verbal tense and aspect manipulations—particularly the present—which bring text and listeners together in one time frame.

This strategy, as has been earlier suggested, is especially useful with respect to *romances* that seek to persuade their audience of a particular point of view. In the texts discussed here, this meant convincing the listeners that customary and officially sanctioned rules of the society in which they lived were followed or broken by the protagonists who guided them through the events and activities of the narrative.

But evaluative language is not unique to the *Romancero del rey don Pedro*. The linguistic mechanisms that allow singers to tell their stories most effectively are present throughout the *Romancero* tradition. They are also, interestingly, found in the work of a royal chronicler who recapitulated some of the texts of the *Romancero del rey don Pedro* for a readership rather than a physically present audience.

The following chapter of this study will take up this subject of ballad language in historical discourse. It will attempt to broaden the scope of the study of evaluative language in the narrative with a discussion of the confrontation between historical and traditional discourse found during the late Middle Ages. The work that will specifically be addressed in these terms is Pero López de Ayala's *Crónica del rey don Pedro*.

5

A Sociolinguistic Approach to
the *Crónica del rey don Pedro*

A. Introduction

In the previous chapter, the relation of evaluative devices in six texts from the *Romancero del rey don Pedro* to the propaganda campaigns of Pedro I of Castile and Enrique de Trastámara was discussed. The conclusion arrived at was that the singers of the *romances*, who were in the employ of both brothers and their descendants, used the remarkable *Romancero* grammar either to point to the King's unfitness for the leadership of Castile or to come to his defense against the Trastámaran accusers. The present chapter will deal also with the propagandistic tendencies of the Pedro texts. This time, however, the evaluative devices of the *Romancero* will be related not to the *guerra civil romancística* of the late Middle Ages, but rather to the written historical propaganda of the medieval chronicler Pero López de Ayala. Ayala, in his *Crónica del rey don Pedro,* appropriates the *romances* dealing with the death of doña Blanca and the appearance of the prophetic *pastor.* He incorporates into his chronicle these traditional versions of events in the years of Pedro's rule for reasons that bear directly on the characteristic linguistic practices of the *Romancero.* Writing at a time when the good, impact-making story relied on tradition—and a traditional version of the past—Ayala used the ballad structure and content to negotiate with his readership the best and most effective path to the conveyance of his own, authorial point of view.[1]

Ayala sought, in his chronicle, to discredit King Pedro. He used the texts from the ballad tradition to give authority to this partisan project. Traditional stories, which have no author, but rather an omniscient narrator who everywhere evaluates the actors and the events of the narrative for the listeners, have an authoritative quality that allows the narrative to directly touch its audience.[2] This is at least partly because of the outstanding use these stories make of vocative and imperative sentences, and also because there is no ironic distance between the author and the teller of a traditional story. These qualities were precisely those that Ayala found in the *Romancero del rey don Pedro*. The *romances* "knew" that King Pedro was an unfit monarch; they "knew" that God had sent warnings to him in the guise of a prophetic shepherd; they "knew" that he had ignored these signals, rendering himself ripe for the type of divine justice he received at the end of his life. Ayala quite shrewdly integrated the authoritative voice of the *Romancero* into his chronicle, using the ballad language to control the attention and imagination of his audience in the same manner as did the ballad singers. The syntactic and lexical manipulations that pointed with maximum effect to King Pedro's tragic course in the *romances* now riveted the minds of readers on the divine prophecy of doom for the King.

Pero López de Ayala, who was a poet, a scholar, a diplomat, and a nobleman who rose to become Chancellor of Castile, had, of course, an authoritative voice of his own. In an era during which learning was still almost an ecclesiastical monopoly,[3] he wrote in the *Crónica* from a unique position of influence. He was learned, well-respected, and important, and his writings were certain to have a significant impact on their audience. Conscious of his privileged position, Ayala wrote with the assurance of a commentator who assumed that:

> the events and decisions of his lifetime would be of enduring importance to Spain and that future generations would look back to this period to find explanations, causes, and insights.[4]

The authority that Ayala borrowed from the oral tradition was ancillary to his own assured judgements. The *romances* from the Pedro cycle added to the *Crónica* an effective means of underscoring the chronicler's point of view. However, to the learned Ayala, the inclusion of ballad material in the chronicle presented the problem of explaining to a readership reliance on *mythos* in an historical account of Pedro's reign. To resolve this inconsistency, Ayala borrowed from the stock of evaluative devices a mechanism which allowed him to deceive his audience into a persuasion that the events of the *romances* were historically accurate. His evaluation of the already highly evaluated *romances* points to some interesting conclusions concerning the confrontation of historical with traditional discourse at the juncture between the written and oral traditions found in the Middle Ages. Here, the *re-creación colectiva* of the *Romancero* assumes one of its most interesting postures as it enters the domain of "private" authorship.

B. The *Crónica* and Its Author

The *Crónica del rey don Pedro*, written by Pero López de Ayala in the last decade of the fourteenth century, is a history of the reign of King Pedro I of Castile. It narrates the events of Pedro's administration, including his dealings with his wife, his mistress, his friends, and his enemies. The *Crónica* is also a disquisition on the circumstances that led to the King's downfall and his death at the hands of his rival half brother. It portrays the moral and psychological aspect of the actors in the drama it describes, demonstrating the political significance of their actions and exposing the types of mentality and the motives of the people who influenced the course of history.

Because of its unusual descriptive and analytical powers, the *Crónica del rey don Pedro* has been considered by many critics to transcend the boundaries between literature and history, and to mark a new era in prose writing for the late Spanish Middle Ages.[5] Menéndez y Pelayo, for example, calls the work "monumento sin par en la historiografía castellana de los tiempos medios."[6] Lapesa writes:

> su obra se caracteriza por manifestar ya rasgos de la nueva orientación, sin desprenderse de las formas artísticas e ideológicas anteriores.[7]

And Américo Castro sees Ayala as "nuestro primer escritor moderno."[8]

The *Crónica del rey don Pedro,* which follows Fernán Sánchez de Valladolid's chronicle of Alfonso XI, does seem to mark a change in the medieval Spanish tradition of royal chronicle writing. For one, unlike some of his predecessors, the author of the *Crónica* was an important figure in the Castilian political scene. His role in the workings of the historical period he wrote about is documented by a career that extended over four reigns and a membership in the Consejo de Regencia. Furthermore, as his profile in the *Generaciones y semblanzas* shows, even among fellow nobles, he was an unusually accomplished statesman who embodied many of the characteristics of the Renaissance ideal of the well-rounded courtier.[9]

Ayala's work was also different in many respects from that of the chroniclers who preceded him. Although, as Diego Catalán has pointed out, he was not the first to combine literary techinique with historical discourse,[10] Ayala succeeded, in the *Crónica del rey don Pedro,* in molding his historical narrative into a dramatic presentation of human destiny that went beyond the descriptive and interpretive abilities of both its predecessor and its immediate successors.[11] With exacting detail, Ayala wrote in the *Crónica* of an atmosphere permeated with violence and fatality, and of a king who finally fell victim to divine justice.

C. Narrative Structure in the *Crónica*

The *Crónica del rey don Pedro* begins with a lengthy account of the death of Alfonso XI, Pedro's father. The pomp and circumstance surrounding the funeral of this respected monarch will later be contrasted with the inglorious end of his imprudent son. Piece by piece, the particulars of the conflicts that led to Pedro's horrible demise are accumulated. The chronicler tells of Pedro's unchivalrous behavior and of the ruthless murders he ordered or committed, including those of his own relatives. He describes the King's disregard for many of his subjects and his cruel behavior towards his wife. He speaks of the warfare between Pedro and the Trastámaran rebels, finally concluding that the regicide which marked the King's downfall resulted from the damage the monarch had inflicted on his own kingdom.

The character and organization of the prose narrative used by Ayala in writing the *Crónica* is, if not entirely new to chronicle composition, an extraordinary treatment of historical material. Ayala does not limit himself to narration in the chronicle. Rather, he intermittently introduces into the work speeches, letters, and dialogues that break the monotony of the prose and add dramatic force to the story. At the same time, however, the narrative structure of the chronicle closely follows the Christian principles of a closed medieval order. The events described in the work, as well as the extra-narrative discourses, are all bound together and given direction by the organizing concept of fate. It is within the rigid framework of a predetermined course that the story of King Pedro unfolds. The temporal order of the work's contents parallels Ayala's final judgement of the monarch, and the narrative structure of the chronicle depends ultimately upon the moral proclaimed in its final section:[1][2]

> E mató muchos en su Regno, por lo qual le vino todo el daño que avedes oido. Por ende diremos aqui lo que dixo el Profeta David: *Agora los Reyes aprended, é sed castigados todos los que juzgades el mundo.* (593)

The diversions from the chronicle's third person narrative that mark Ayala's work as a departure from most previous historical accounts almost always develop logically from the historical relation in progress. For example, in chapter 11 of the Año Cuarto (1353), Ayala relates the fracas surrounding Pedro's desertion of Queen Blanca immediately following their marriage for María de Padilla. He first sets the scene in narrative form:

> Luego el miércoles siguiente despues de las bodas el Rey comia en su palacio en las casas del Abad de Santander dó él posaba. . . . E estando el rey á la mesa llegaron á él la Reyna Doña Maria su madre, é la Reyna Doña Leonor su tia. (433)

Ayala then interrupts the narrative to quote directly the plea made to Pedro by his mother and his aunt, imploring him to stay away from María de Padilla:

> "Señor, á nos es dicho que vos paredes luego partir de aqui para dó esta Doña Maria de Padilla: é pedimos vos por merced que non lo querades facer." (433)

In chapter 17 of the Año Onceno (1360), Ayala interrupts the narrative describing the murder of one of the King's vassals, Gutier Ferrández de Toledo, to introduce into the third person account a letter from the luckless victim. He begins the passage by reporting the circumstances of the scene:

> Este dia, estando el dicho Gutier Ferrandez preso en la posada del Maestre de Santiago, dixo . . . que queria enviar una carta al Rey. (507)

Then he develops the situation further by inserting the actual contents of the letter:

> "Señor: Yo Gutier Ferrandez de Toledo beso vuestras manos, é me despido de la vuestra merced, é vó para otro Señor." (507)

In both of the above examples, the nonnarrative passages evolve logically from the prose sections that precede them. The same is true of other interruptions in the chronicle's narrative, where incidental material is similarly integrated into the main body of the work. There are, however, two occasions during the course of the *Crónica del rey don Pedro* on which Ayala deviates from this practice.[13] Interestingly, in both cases the nonintegrated material derives from the *Romancero del rey don Pedro*. The first such deviation occurs in the eleventh year of the chronicle. Ayala abruptly introduces into the narrative the story of a *clérigo profeta* who prophesies adversity for the King.[14] The second is the familiar tale of the *pastorcico profeta* and the death of doña Blanca examined in chapter 4 of this study. Both stories in the chronicle bear a striking resemblance to their *Romancero* forebears. In fact, as Entwistle has pointed out, Ayala's prose accounts even mimic the ballad assonance pattern, with "three or four assonances in the series Ó or Ó-E" (312) in the *pastor* segment and an A-O model in the *clérigo* case (315). It seems likely that the historian was familiar with the *romances* hostile to King Pedro and borrowed from them in his own composition.

D. The *Romancero* in the *Crónica del rey don Pedro*

In both the *clérigo profeta* and the *pastorcico profeta* stories as related in the chronicle, the King is warned of a divine mandate for his demise. He is told that unless he alters his behavior, he will lose his throne and his kingdom. In each instance, the King reacts immediately to discredit the warning he has received, refusing to believe its divine origin. In the *clérigo profeta* story, he insists that the cleric who prophesies his doom is acting as the agent of some adversary. Even when the cleric protests, maintaining that the warning comes from Santo Domingo and that he acts only as an intermediary, the King refuses to heed his message. In the *pastorcico profeta* tale, the King is also told that his end is divinely willed. Like the *clérigo*'s warning, the *pastor*'s alarm refers to the King's malevolent behavior and promises avoidance of the evil prophecy if the monarch agrees to reform. Again, Pedro looks for a mortal instigator of this prophecy, rejecting all evidence that the warning is a reflection of God's will.

Of the two traditional stories recounted in Ayala's *Crónica,* it is the *pastorcico profeta* tale that contains the more striking deviation from the logical structure—and content—of the chronicle. Unlike the earthly cleric, who dreams his prophecy and who, as his death by burning on Pedro's orders demonstrates, receives no special protection from God, the *pastorcico profeta* is an otherworldly creature taken by everyone to be divinely ordained. He appears from nowhere and then, just as mysteriously, disappears into oblivion. Dissimilar also to the *clérigo* segment, which is framed in the chronicle by the main action of the chapter in which it is told, the facts of the visionary appearance of the prophetic shepherd are recorded by Ayala as an addendum to the action—neither separate from, nor arising logically out of, the principal transactions described in the narrative. In fact, the *pastorcico profeta* story directly confronts the logical sequence of events in the chronologically ordered history. It is preceded in the chronicle by the announcement of the death of Pedro's wife, Queen Blanca. Ayala reports that the King contracted with a certain *ballestero* to carry out his order for Blanca's death after her guard, Iñigo Ortiz de Estúñiga, refused to do the deed. Without stating precisely how Blanca died, he comments, "E pesó mucho dello á todos los del Regno despues que lo sopieron é vino por ende mucho mal a Castilla" (512). The story of the *pastorcico profeta* then follows the account of Blanca's death. It comes as something of a surprise as the warning to Pedro to return to his wife or to face certain punishment clearly predates the Queen's demise:

```
1   E acaesció que un dia,
2   estando ella en la prision dó morió,
3   llegó un ome que parescia pastor,
4   é fué al Rey Don Pedro dó andaba á
        caza en aquella comarca de Xerés
        é de Medina do la Reyna estaba presa,
5   é dixole, que Dios le enviaba decir
6   que fuese cierto que el mal que él
        facia á la Reyna Doña Blanca su muger
7   que le avia de ser muy acaloñado,
8   é que en esto non pusiese dubda;
9   pero si quisiese tornar á ella,
10  é facer su vida como debia,
11  que avria della fijo que heredase
        su Regno.
```

12 E el Rey fué muy espantado,
13 é fizo prender el ome que esto le dixo,
14 é tovo que la Reyna Doña Blanca le
      enviaba decir estas palabras:
15 é luego envió á Martin Lopez de
      Cordoba, su Camarero
16 é á Matheos Ferrandez, su Chanciller
      del sello de la poridad, á Medina Sidonia
      dó la Reyna estaba presa,
17 á que ficiesen pesquisa cómo veniera
      aquel ome,
18 é si le enviára la Reyna.
19 E llegaron sin sospecha á la villa
20 é fueron luego á do la Reyna yacia
      en prision en una torre,
21 é fallaronla que estaba las rodillas
      en tierra
22 é faciendo oracion;
23 é cuidó que la iban á matar
24 é lloraba,
25 é acomendóse é Dios.
26 E ellos le dixeron, que el Rey queria
      saber de un ome que le fuera á decir ciertas
      palabras cómo fuera,
27 é por cuyo mandado:
28 é preguntaronle si ella le enviára;
29 é ella dixo, que nunca tal ome viera.
30 Otrosi las guardas que estaban
31 y, que la tenian presa,
32 dixeron que non podria ser
      que la Reyna enviase tal ome,
33 ca nunca dexaban á ningund ome entrar
      dó ella estaba.
34 E segund esto paresce que fué obra de Dios,
35 é asi lo tovieron todos los que le vieron
36 é oyeron.
37 E el ome estovo preso algunos dias,
38 é despues soltaronle,
39 é nunca mas dél sopieron. (512-13)

The curious detail of the illogical sequence of events reported in the third chapter of the twelfth year (1361) of the *Crónica* is that Ayala never directly links the *pastor* incident with the Queen's death. The traditional account, on the other hand, more logically juxtaposes the two events. As discussed in chapter 4 of this study, at least one of the *romances* concerning the *pastorcico profeta* clearly presents the Queen's murder as an attempt by the King to avert the evil portended by the *pastor*'s prophecy.[15] Ayala, whose standard of logic and reason in the chronicle is here transgressed, seems merely to have added the details of popular apocrypha for maximum effect at a pivotal moment in the narrative. He makes no attempt to reconcile the facts of Blanca's death with the shepherd's warning. He does not, like the *romance,* claim cause and effect for the two events. Rather, he allows the traditional story of the prophetic shepherd to evaluate for him Pedro's involvement in the unhappy circumstances of Blanca's life as well as his complicity in the loss of his own throne.

E. Evaluation in the *Crónica*

By introducing into his history two popular oral versions of the events of Pedro's reign, Ayala succeeds, in the *Crónica,* in underscoring for his audience the central thesis of his composition in a maximally tellable way. There are several reasons for this success. First of all, the *romances* that Ayala used in the chronicle provided his audience with a familiar relation of the events of Pedro's rule. It is most probable that by the time Ayala wrote the chronicle, the *romances* hostile to King Pedro had become well known throughout Castile.[16] The Trastámaran camp, which had commissioned many of these ballads, undoubtedly encouraged their transmission—both to gain support for its war and to legitimize its overthrow of the legal monarch. The repeated singing of the anti-Pedro propaganda would then prior to the chronicle's composition have established and reinforced the version of Pedro's rule that pointed to the King's recalcitrance in making amends and following God's law. This, of course, was Ayala's interpretation as well, and by introducing the familiar relation into his history, he corroborated his own imputation of the King with the widely accepted "facts" of the defeated monarch's reign.

Secondly, the *romances* that Ayala used served to explicate his central thesis in the chronicle. They explained the tragedy of King Pedro by referring the audience to events that effectively demonstrated the monarch's stubborn refusal to heed God's word. The introduction of the story of the shepherd's prophecy *after* the report of Blanca's death, for example, functioned to suspend the action of the chronicle's narrative while the readers' attention was transferred back in time to the warning Pedro had received with respect to his harsh treatment of the Queen. The result was a powerful reminder of the fact that a king needed God's aid in order to govern in justice and right reason. Pedro, who did not know or fear God, was unable to enforce justice in society, thus failing in his responsibility towards his family, his people, and God.

A third important function of the *romances* within the context of the chronicle was to allow Ayala to justify the treachery of the renegade nobility in the overthrow of the legitimate king and to exonerate his Trastámaran successors of their involvement in the regicide that ended his reign. Ayala was himself a deserter from King Pedro's side. For seventeen years a loyal supporter of Pedro's reign, he became disenchanted with the King and finally left him for the forces of Enrique de Trastámara.[17] Ensconced in the succesful Trastámaran camp years later, he recorded the events of Pedro's rule with the self-serving purpose of excusing his own behavior towards the legitimate ruler and justifying the oath of loyalty he gave to the illegitimate pretender. He had to demonstrate in the chronicle a moral imperative behind the regicide that brought the Trastámarans to the throne and to rationalize the benefits that accrued to him and to his family through his involvement in the Trastámaran coup.[18] The *romances* that he appropriated in the chronicle provided him with a highly effective means of succeeding in this endeavor.

The *romances* said, in effect, that Pedro was a bad king, and that it was his inability to live up to the high standard of behavior expected of a monarch that led to his tragic death. God appeared in the *romances* in the form of the *pastorcico profeta* to reinforce this idea and to make clear Pedro's deficiencies by showing the King at his least attractive—i.e., conspiring to have the innocent Queen Blanca murdered in an attempt to avert the punishment predicted for him by the divine shepherd. However, it should be pointed out that this dramatic story content was not the only component of Ayala's case against Pedro borrowed from the *Romancero*. Ayala recapitulated in the chronicle both the general content of the *romances* and the very linguistic and structural elements of the traditional stories. In so doing, he made his argument for the downfall of the monarch who flagrantly ignored God's warnings maximally persuasive.

The *pastorcico profeta* story in the chronicle begins with an Abstract/ Orientation section that outlines the basic details of the encounter between Pedro and the supernatural shepherd:

1 E acaesció que un dia,
2 estando ella en la prision dó morió,
3 llegó un ome que parescia pastor,
4 é fué al Rey Don Pedro dó andaba
     á caza en aquella comarca de
     Xerés é de Medina do la Reyna
     estaba presa.

It proceeds with a Complicating Action section (5-20) which relates the substance of the interview between Pedro and the shepherd and the subsequent *pesquisa* ordered by the King to ascertain Queen Blanca's role in the strange events. An Evaluation of this role then follows: in a heartrending description of the Queen's unhappy situation—e.g., "estaba las rodillas en tierra é faciendo oración . . . é lloraba, é acomendóse á Dios" (21-25)—Ayala, using the language of the *romances,* interprets for the audience the true posture of the Queen with respect to Pedro's downfall. She is a pious and innocent victim of the King's injustices, and a witness to his evil and ungodly nature. An extension of the Evaluation in lines 30-36 is, as will later be shown, a rationalization for the introduction of the *pastoricico profeta* story into the history. It confirms for the audience the "historicity" of the *romance* with the addition of personal testimony to the veracity of the traditional account.

The Resolution of the *pastorcico profeta* tale lies outside the lines of the unusual story. It may be found in Ayala's statement of the Queen's death which precedes the *pastorcico* tale and in the *romance* which makes overt the connection between the death of doña Blanca and the shepherd's appearance:

> ...   Mandó matar a la reina
> ese día a un caballero,   pareciéndole acababa
> con su muerte el mal agüero.
>
> (28b-30, text 66)

It is interesting to note that Ayala refrains in this section of the chronicle, as he does elsewhere, from making explicit the relation between Pedro's wrongdoing and Blanca's death. In the passage which tells of Blanca's death, for example, he writes, "E el Rey mandó á un ome . . . que diese hierbas á la Reyna con que moriese" (512). But he notes that the King's command was not carried out by this *ome,* so the connection between the Queen's eventual death and Pedro's order is never articulated. Ayala counts on the audience's foreknowledge of the ballad to evaluate for him the link between the King's strange encounter with the *pastorcico profeta* and the Queen's subsequent demise. He can do this because the audience for the chronicle was the same as for the ballad. The *Crónica,* although a written work, was a vernacular history and as such, was an extension of the tradition of the spoken word.[19] It was, moreover, easy to read and, as the fourteen extant manuscripts indicate, widely distributed among Spaniards.[20] A Coda, evinced in the last lines of the *pastorcico profeta* story, brings the narrative up-to-date with the information that the *pastor* was freed, never to be heard from again (37-38).

Like the *Romancero,* evaluation in the chronicle's *pastorcico profeta* story is found in nearly every line of the narrative. In the *Crónica,* however, the comparators, correlatives, and explicatives of the *romances* are used both to evaluate the events and actions of the chronicle story and to reformulate the traditional tale within the confines of historical prose writing. Thus Ayala converts the *romances* into a gloss on the history as a whole. For example, although told in the third person, the chronicle version maintains the same threatening language of the *pastor*'s address to Pedro in the *romances. Si* clauses—e.g., "si quisiese tornar á ella, é facer su vida como debia, que avria della fijo que heredase su Regno" (9-11)—mimic the choice between success and tragedy offered the King through the words of the *pastor* in the *romances*: "Si quieres volver con ella, / darte ha Dios un heredero" (24b-25a, text 66). In the chronicle, however, such comparators also interpret for the reader the biblical reference stated in the final section of the historical work: *"Agora los Reyes aprended, é sed castigados todos los que juzgades el mundo"* (593). A negative clause in the chronicle, also spoken by the *pastorcico profeta*, menaces the King with the promise of future punishment for his reprehensible conduct towards the Queen—"é que en esto non pusiese dubda" (8)—just as it does in the *romance* version: "por cierto sepas   te vendrá desmán por ello" (24a-24b, text 66a). But in the chronicle, this comparator points also to the actual punishment meted out to Pedro, as described in the history's last argument: "E mató muchos en su Regno, por lo qual le vino todo el daño que avedes oido" (593). An explicative, often used in oral narrative to transfer the listeners' attention backward and forward in time, is inserted into the chronicle account to remind the readership that it was God who reinforced social justice, and that Pedro would ultimately have Him to reckon with: "E segund esto paresce que fué obra de Dios" (34). This, of course, is the central thesis of Ayala's argument in his relation of the events of Pedro's rule.

Other evaluative devices function in the chronicle, as in the *Romancero*, purely for dramatic effect. For example, the use of imperfect and progressive verbal forms to position the audience within the circumstances of the story, a technique generally considered characteristic of the oral literary situation, is carried over into the *Crónica* for the purpose of involving the reader in the pathos of the chronicle's drama—e.g., "estando ella en la prisión dó morió" (2), "estaba las rodillas en tierra é faciendo oración" (21-22), and "é cuidó que la iban á matar é lloraba" (23-24).

Historical detail and traditional anecdote are combined in Ayala's chronicle for the purposes of telling an effective story that reinforced the writer's point of view. The historian used the *romances* concerning the death of doña Blanca and the appearance of the prophetic shepherd to dramatize the confrontation of divine forces with an unyielding, wrongdoing king. Against the backdrop of the tragic death of the innocent queen, the *romance* stories pointed in the chronicle to the King's uncharitable attitudes and to his consequential inability to gain divine sanction for the monarchal role he played. This was precisely the effect Ayala sought in the chronicle, yet the problem remained for the historian to compensate for the apparently fictional character of the story of the supernatural *pastor* who prophesied the King's downfall.

Within the context of the *Romancero*, neither prophecies nor supernatural creatures are commonplace.[21] Within the confines of Ayala's chronicle, however, the supernatural occurrence seems even less probable. For one, Ayala claimed recourse in the chronicle to only the most scrupulous of authorities. He did not consider the mnemonic tradition—from which his knowledge of the *romances* undoubtedly came[22]–to be among those good authorities. Indeed, he takes care in a prologue to the work to stress his antipathy for the unreliable *flaca memoria* of human beings.[23] He writes:

> La memoria de los omes es muy flaca, é non se puede acordar de todas las cosas que en el tiempo pasado acaescieron. (399)

and

> yo Pero Lopez de Ayala, con el ayuda de Dios, lo entiendo continuar asi lo mas verdaderamente que pudiere de lo que ví, en lo qual non entiendo decir sinon verdad: otrosi de lo que acaesce en mi edad é en mi tiempo en algunas partidas donde yo non he estado, é lo supiere por verdadera relacion de Señores é Caballeros, é otros dignos de fé é de creer, de quienes lo oí, é me dieron dende testimonio, tomandolo con la mayor diligencia que yo pude. (400)

For another, it seems unlikely that Ayala himself believed in the divine origin of the prophetic shepherd.[24] On the contrary, his account of the supernatural *pastor* likens the character to an earthly creature capable of arrest and interrogation by the Castilian authorities.

Because of his early promise to rely on "good authority" in the chronicle and his own penchant for logical and rational explanation, Ayala needed in his work to somehow authenticate the supernatural *pastor* and the story of his appearance gleaned from the oral tradition. Ayala did not ask or expect from his readers a willing suspension of disbelief as a writer of fiction might do. Rather, he developed an intricate network of "neutral" observers in the chronicle whose evaluative comments he embedded into the narrative in order to insist that the traditional story was in fact of historical validity. According to Ayala, these third person characters actually "saw" and "heard" the entire exchange between Pedro and the supernatural *pastor,* and they witnessed as well the aftermath of the incident. No fewer than four times during the course of the short passage concerning the arrival and disappearance of the otherworldly creature does Ayala introduce these neutral observers of the story's action to evaluate for the reader the strange occurrence and its consequences. In the first instance, Ayala interposes the figures of Martín López de Córdoba and Matheos Ferrández, the King's counselors, who see the Queen kneeling on the ground and praying (21-22). In the second instance, Ayala admits the commentary of the Queen's guards into the story. These third person characters say that the Queen could not possibly be responsible for the *pastor*'s confrontation with the King, for they allowed no one to visit her cell (30-33). In the third case, Ayala adds the evaluation of many unnamed eyewitness observers who proclaim the *pastor*'s nature to be divine. These observers, "que le vieron é oyeron" (35-36), agree with Ayala's own evaluation of the strange event as "obra de Dios." In the fourth and final instance, Ayala again uses unnamed subjects. This is perhaps the most interesting case of evaluation, for it involves an attempt by Ayala to make the supernatural event almost commonplace. He writes that "they" freed the *pastor*, never to find out anything further about him: "soltáronle, é nunca mas dél sopieron" (38-39). The notion that the unearthly creature could have been successfully captured and imprisoned by the authorities suggests that this *pastor* was perhaps more a divinely inspired messenger, on the style of the *clérigo profeta*, than a truly divine incarnation. In any case, it reduces the traditional *pastorcico profeta*, who in the *romances* is quite clearly an unearthly creation,[25] to more human and rational terms.

Entwistle, in his commentary on Ayala's curious embellishment of the traditional *pastor* tale, claims that the historian

> is unconvincingly rational when he declares the prophet to be capable of arrest and temporary imprisonment and claims to give details of the committee of enquiry. (312)

Yet is seems that Ayala, in his syntactic structuring of the *pastor* tale, has effectively precluded this argument. Ayala's version of the *pastorcico profeta* story is convincing, as is his rationalization of the unworldly creature, because it is told within a historical framework which draws upon trustworthy eye-witness observers—who in some cases are historically accurate personalities (e.g., Martín López de Córdoba and Matheos Ferrández)—to give evidence for the historical validity of the incident. Ayala very shrewdly does not attribute any of the evaluative commentary to himself. In quoting the comments of neutral observers, rather than insisting upon the authorial point of view, he more dramatically reiterates the point he wishes to make in the chronicle as a whole. Ayala, who throughout refrains from overtly condemning the legitimate ruler, instead forces his readers to make moral and political judgements on the basis of the material he presents (Nader 25). By supplying his audience with a ready evaluation of the contents of the chronicle, Ayala disarms his readers, persuading them to accept as generally true what is in fact a poetic version of King Pedro's rule. The result is a reformulation of the *romances* in historical prose. He thus reworks the "fictitious" poetry into "veracious" prose.

F. Historical and Traditional Discourse in the *Crónica*

The *Crónica del rey don Pedro* is an interesting example of the use of evaluated narratives for evaluative purposes in an authoritative historical work. The appropriation of *Romancero* texts and ballad language in the *Crónica del rey don Pedro* demonstrates that the historian, Pero López de

Ayala, recognized the highly persuasive character of traditional stories and used them to evaluate his own version of the years of King Pedro's rule. Moreover, employing the evaluative devices most fitting in an historical context (i.e., third person evaluation), he embedded into his narrative a mixture of the *Romance de la muerte de la reina Blanca* and the *Romance del pastorcico profeta* in order to offer an explanation for a past that included his own treachery against the legitimate king.

It seems that Ayala very discerningly "shopped" through the oral tradition when preparing his chronicle, choosing to rely on traditional discourse—which he otherwise eschewed—only when that discourse effectively articulated his own position as an interested historian. Ayala's task, which was to assemble the evidence against Pedro in a most convincing manner, was in fact greatly helped by this selective shopping. By choosing well-known *romances* that depicted Pedro as deficient in the very criteria for monarchal rule dictated by Castilian law and custom, Ayala was able to support his thesis that it was Pedro's failures as a king—and not the political intrigues of the Trastámaran camp—that caused the legal heir to the Castilian throne to be deposed. Ayala also was careful to select *romances* for use in the chronicle that spelled out divine justice as a reason for Pedro's demise. It was not simply the will of the people, these *romances* said, but more importantly, the will of God that Pedro should be dethroned. Furthermore, Ayala chose *romances* that portrayed Queen Blanca in the most favorable of lights. Blanca, a rallying point in the anti-Pedro oral historical propaganda, was selected by Ayala to perpetuate the tradition hostile to the dethroned king. She thus became in the chronicle, as in the *Romancero,* a central figure in the post-facto justification of the Trastámaran coup.

In this manner, the *Romancero* provided Ayala with several cogent, popular arguments against the King, and their incorporation into the chronicle invested the historian's written propaganda with a more potent kind of authority. Indeed, instead of confronting the historical discourse of the chronicle with its traditional locutions, the *Romancero,* through its incorporation into the history, encouraged a single, unavoidable interpretation of the years of Pedro's rule. The *romances* that Ayala selected—which were all hostile to King Pedro— corroborated, supported, and reinforced his version of Castilian history, while the chronicle recorded for posterity an indelible, authoritative edition of the oral historical propaganda. As Entwistle notes, both singers and listeners since Ayala's time have had a "standard" in the *Crónica* which they carefully consulted in producing and reproducing the *pastorcico profeta* story (312). Ayala was not the first, or only, chronicler to rework traditional material into historical prose writing,[26] but perhaps he was one of the first to do so as part of a conscious narrative strategy. Ayala, it may be noted, was successful in this strategy, for the *Crónica del rey don Pedro* scrupulously preserved the *romances* most damaging to Pedro's image (i.e., those that showed the King doing battle with even God's messengers), impressing the hostile, yet potentially alterable, *romances* into a mold that could not be changed.

6

Conclusion

A sociolinguistic approach to the language of the *Romancero* addresses two important issues in the study of the production and reproduction of *romances* within different historical, geographical, and social situations. First of all, it considers the role of literature in the promotion and formation of attitudes and beliefs that draw members of a society together in solidarity. Secondly, it discusses the relation between these attitudes and the language through which their promotion and formation are effected. It treats the characteristic patterning of *Romancero* grammar as an evaluative strategy, or a means through which audience interest and sympathy may be captured and maintained within a variety of oral literary situations. Thus the negative and interrogative constructions, verbal tense and aspect manipulations, dialogue and soliloquy, and so forth, that are common to the linguistic structure of the *romances* are seen as instruments in the establishment and articulation of the group dynamic which is vital to the *re-creación colectiva* of the *Romancero*. They are the media through which the singer collaborates with the listeners, who exercise an immediate and ongoing control over the performance, to shape the *romance* into a statement of the common interests and aspirations of the group. They call attention to various events and activities in the text, departing from basic narrative syntax—or the sequence of verbal clauses matching the sequence of events described—with a regularity which complements the special requirements of the face-to-face situation of an oral performance where there is no turning back the page.

The use of evaluative language to establish immediate channels of communication between singer and listener in the oral literary situation is particularly evident in the *romances noticieros*. In these compositions, the singers (who frequently functioned as mediators in the sociopolitical mission of the State or its opponents) drew upon the attitudes and beliefs of their audiences to shape the language of their texts into an evaluation of contemporary political circumstances and activities. In the *Romancero del rey don Pedro*, for example, dialogue between various actors in the drama of fourteenth-century Castilian politics guided the listeners through the events of the fratricidal struggle between King Pedro I of Castile and his half brother Enrique de Trastámara. Other linguistic devices similarly evaluated the activities of the turbulent period, shaping the anti-Pedro *romances* into a harsh indictment of the dethroned king which later found its way into a royal chronicle, the *Crónica del rey don Pedro,* preserving for posterity the insidious locutions of the hostile propaganda. The *romances,* and later the chronicle, served to legitimize the fratricide which brought the Trastámaras to the throne. Drawing upon custom and officially established legal codes, they cast the Trastámaran coup in a religious and moral light, insinuating through the ballad structure Pedro's unfitness for the leadership of Castile and a divine mandate for his replacement by Enrique.

But evaluative language is by no means unique to the *romances noticieros.* Singers of any oral text have constantly to maintain a kind of communicative activity with their audiences during performance, and this communicative activity is implicit in the very linguistic structures used to produce and transmit the *Romancero* tradition as a whole. Thus in the Carolingian and novelesque, as well as the historical, *romances,* singers regularly draw upon a catalogue of evaluative devices in order to perform their compositions most effectively and memorably, underscoring for their listeners the tellability of the *romances* within a variety of oral literary situations. These devices, which say to the audience, "The events of this text are truly worthy of report," lend to the *Romancero* its characteristic patterning of language—a patterning which is not simply a stylistic feature of the *romances,* but perhaps more importantly, an essential aspect of its very *tradicionalidad.* While the medieval Spanish *juglares* may have used evaluative devices to capture and maintain audience interest, as well as to make clear the point of a story's content, the transmitters of the *romances* have also to use linguistic strategies to rework the archaic texts within settings that may be remote from the social, historical, and geographical framework of the Spanish Middle Ages. The result is an open-ended tradition which throughout centuries of collective re-creation has led to a perpetuation of the poetic and ideological legacy of medieval Spain.

Thus the type of analysis presented in this study of the grammar of the *romances noticieros* in the *Romancero del rey don Pedro* may be extended to include other kinds of *romances* which do not so directly deal with the history and politics of the period in which they are produced or transmitted. These other *romances* use evaluative language in ways similar to the *Romancero del rey don Pedro,* but their evaluative thrust may be directed towards different circumstances and situations. These are the concrete details that lead singers to come to varying decisions in the structuring of their compositions. But a contextual approach to the *Romancero* tradition and to the language of which it is composed goes beyond this surface level relation. By considering literature in terms of the role it plays in society, and language in terms of its affinity to the attitudes and beliefs of different groups, a socio-linguistic approach to language in the *Romancero* takes an important step towards uncovering the sometimes barely conscious postulates that lie beneath the surface of narrative structure. It is in effect through the language of evaluation that the concrete daily social behavior of the members of a society may be linked with the catalogue of abstract values that are perpetuated across the boundaries of time, geography, and culture through the production and reproduction of the *Romancero*. This is a fundamental underpinning of the tradition "que vive en variantes," and through a clearer understanding of this underpinning, a more intelligible concept of the literature and of the times may be gained.

Notes

Chapter 1: Introduction

[1] Diego Catalán, *Siete siglos de romancero* (Madrid: Gredos, 1969) 95-99. See also, Angus MacKay, "The Ballad and the Frontier in Late Mediaeval Spain," *BHS* 53 (1976): 16.

[2] The *canto aguinaldero,* as Catalán and MacKay point out, corresponds to a Christmas folk custom "whereby youths elect a 'king' and 'queen' during the Christmas festivities and go from house to house collecting presents (*aguinaldo*)" (MacKay 16). The older text recalled by the *aguinaldero* is the *Romance de don Fadrique, Maestre de Santiago.* The following lines—from Marcelino Menéndez y Pelayo's *Antología de poetas líricos castellanos,* 14 vols. (Madrid: Sucesores de Hernando, 1916-24) 8: 125—are instructive:

> —Venid acá, mis porteros   hágase lo que he mandado.—
> Aun no lo hubo bien dicho,   la cabeza le han cortado
> a doña María de Padilla   en un plato la ha enviado.

For additional information and discussion of this *romance,* see Antonio Pérez-Gómez, *Romancero del rey don Pedro* (Valencia: La Fonte Que Mana y Corre, 1954) 40-41, 100-13.

[3] The use of the term *ideology* in this study refers to the practices, rituals, and apparatuses that represent the relations of individuals to their conditions of existence. The *romances,* as they are sung by their transmitters, articulate a simulation of these relations within particular social and historical circumstances. At the same time, however, the *romances* maintain on some deeper level the model of their medieval prototypes. A useful discussion of ideology in this sense may be found in Louis Althusser, "Ideology and Ideological State Apparatuses (Notes towards an Investigation)," *Lenin and Philosophy* (New York and London: Monthly Review, 1971) 127-86.

[4] Diego Catalán, "Los modos de producción y 'reproducción' del texto literario y la noción de apertura," *Homenaje a Julio Caro Baroja* (Madrid: Centro de Investigaciones Sociológicas, 1978) 246. See also Samuel G. Armistead, "Epic and Ballad: A Tradionalist Perspective," *Olifant* 8.4 (Summer 1981): 376-88.

[5] William J. Entwistle, "The *Romancero del Rey Don Pedro* in Ayala and the *Cuarta Crónica General,*" *MLR* 25 (1930): 310.

⁶ Colin Smith, *Spanish Ballads* (1964; Oxford: Pergamon, 1971), notes:

At the opening of a ballad we are often taken up bodily and plunged into an action
that is already well under way, suddenly immersed in its total atmosphere. (32)

⁷ Catalán, "Los modos," uses this term to describe the open-endedness of the ballad
tradition.

⁸ Ramón Menéndez Pidal, *Romancero hispánico (hispano-portugués, americano y
sefardí): teoría e historia,* 2nd ed., 2 vols. (Madrid: Espasa-Calpe, 1968) 2: 4.

⁹ William Labov, *Language in the Inner City* (Philadelphia: U of Pennsylvania P)
370.

¹⁰ The story of María's bloodthirstiness in the *aguinaldero* is itself an example of the
capacity for this tale to be introduced into a variety of contexts. María's strange request
is a clear echo of a biblical tale in which Salome, daughter of Herod, asks for the gift
of John the Baptist's head.

¹¹ For example, Andrés de Claramonte's play *De esta agua no beberé,* Lope de Vega's
plays *La carbonera* and *La corona merecida,* and Pero López de Ayala's *Crónica del rey
don Pedro* (to be discussed in chapter 5 of this study). For further discussion, see J. R.
Lomba y Pedraja, "El rey don Pedro en el teatro," *Homenaje a Menéndez y Pelayo en el
año vigésimo de su profesoriado,* 2 vols. (Madrid, 1899) 2: 257-339; Marcelino Menéndez
y Pelayo, *Estudios sobre el teatro de Lope de Vega,* 6 vols. (Santander: Aldus, S. A. de
Artes Gráficas, 1949) vol. 4; Entwistle; Menéndez y Pelayo, *Antología* 12: 110-57; and
Ramón Menéndez Pidal, "Relatos poéticos en las crónicas medievales," *RFE* 10 (1923):
329-72.

¹² G. H. Bower, "Experiments on Story Understanding and Recall," *Quarterly Journal
of Experimental Psychology* 28 (1976): 511-34. Also, Jean M. Mandler and Nancy S.
Johnson, "Remembrance of Things Parsed: Story Structure and Recall," *Cognitive
Psychology* 9 (1977): 111-51; Perry W. Thorndyke, "Cognitive Structures in Compre-
hension and Memory of Narrative Discourse," *Cognitive Psychology* 9 (1977): 77-110;
Angela Hildyare and David R. Olson, "On the Comprehension and Memory of Oral Vs.
Written Discourse," in Deborah Tannen, ed., *Spoken and Written Discourse: Exploring
Orality and Literacy* (Norwood, NJ: Ablex, 1982) 19-33.

¹³ Ruth House Webber, *Formulistic Diction in the Spanish Ballad* (Berkeley: U of
California P, 1951), gives a thorough discussion of this approach. See also Webber,
"Lenguaje tradicional: epopeya y romancero," *Actas del Sexto Congreso de Hispanistas*
(Toronto: U of Toronto P, 1980) 779-82; Webber, "Prologomena to the Study of the
Narrative Structure of the Hispanic Ballad," *Ballads and Ballad Research,* Selected papers
of the International Conference on Nordic and Anglo-American Ballad Research (Seattle:
U of Washington P, 1978) 221-30; and John S. Miletich, "Narrative Style in Spanish and
Slavic Traditional Narrative Poetry: Implications for the Study of Romance Epic," *Olifant*
2.2 (1974): 109-28.

¹⁴ Catalán, "Los modos," provides an excellent discussion of "deep structures" in the
Romancero. See also Catalán, "Análisis semiótico de estructuras abiertas: el modelo
'Romancero,'" *RH: Poética* 231-49; Catalán, J. Antonio Cid, Beatriz Mariscal, Flor

Salazar, Ana Valenciano, and Sandra Robertson, *Catálogo General del Romancero*, 3 vols. (Madrid: S.M.P., 1982-84); Samuel G. Armistead, "Current Trends in *Romancero* Research," *La Corónica* 12.1 (1983): 4; Cesare Segre, *Le strutture e il tempo: narrazione, poesia, modelli* (Torino: Ernandi, 1974); A. J. Greimas, *Sémantique structurale* (Paris: Larousse, 1966); Claude Brémond, *Logic du récit* (Paris: Seuil, 1973). It should be noted that the theory of deep structures in narrative derives from the transformation-generative grammar developed by Noam Chomsky in *Syntactic Structures* (The Hague: Mouton, 1957) and modified in *Aspects of the Theory of Syntax* (Cambridge, MA: MIT P, 1965).

[15] "Tellability," for Labov, is the capacity of a narrative to be reported so that it is not met, as pointless stories in English are, with the "withering rejoinder, 'So what?' " (Labov 366).

[16] D. W. Foster, "A Note on the Rhetorical Structure of the Ballad *Alora la bien cercada,*" *RN* 15 (1973): 392-96, discusses this problem.

[17] The texts of the *Romancero del rey don Pedro*—to be discussed in chapter 4 of this study—are outstanding examples of the use of the *noticieros* for political propaganda.

[18] See Catalán, *Siete siglos* 81.

[19] S. G. Morley, *Spanish Ballads* (New York: Holt, 1911) 127, for example, calls Pedro's rule, as seen through the *romances,* "a black reign."

[20] Menéndez y Pelayo, *Antología* 8: 134-36, texts 68 and 68a. The texts used in this study are from Marcelino Menéndez y Pelayo's *Antología,* vol. 8; rpt. with apendices from F. J. Wolf and C. Hofmann, *Primavera y flor de romances* (Berlin, 1856). Numbers used to identify each text are from *Primavera.* For further bibliographical information, see Pérez-Gómez. For textual analyses and discussion, see chapter 4 of this study.

[21] Menéndez y Pelayo, *Antología* 8: 126-29, texts 66 and 66a.

[22] Menéndez y Pelayo, *Antología* 8: 131-33, text 67a.

[23] Menéndez y Pelayo, *Antología* 8: 129-31, text 67.

[24] See chapter 2 of this study for discussion.

[25] See chapter 4 of this study for discussion.

[26] For example, Pérez-Gómez, Entwistle, and Menéndez y Pelayo. The most recent *Bibliografía crítica del Romancero* (1979-83), prepared by Samuel G. Armistead and kindly made available to me by him in typescript form, indicates that current studies of these ballads are scarce and that to date, no systematic study of language in the *Romancero del rey don Pedro* has been attempted, save this author's 1980 PhD dissertation ("The Language of Evaluation: A Sociolinguistic Approach to Narrative Structure in the 'Romancero del rey don Pedro' and in Pero López de Ayala's 'Crónica del rey don Pedro,' " Stanford U). Yet, as references to the *Romancero del rey don Pedro* in works such as Joseph Szertics's *Tiempo y verbo en el Romancero Viejo* (Madrid: Gredos, 1967) indicate, it is rich in the types of structures considered characteristic of the Spanish ballad tradition.

[27] Menéndez Pidal, "Relatos poéticos" 372.

Chapter 2: The Language of the *Romancero*

[1] The notion of *aspect* has been somewhat troublesome to linguists. The term has been used to refer to a number of different grammatical concepts, including flexion, perfective and imperfective verbs, and derivative morphemes. The term will be used here, along with *tense,* primarily to note the difference in Spanish between the imperfect and the preterite, which respectively express actions in progress and actions which have been concluded.

[2] This text is from Marcelino Menéndez y Pelayo, *Antología,* vol. 8, text 132.

[3] Rafael Lapesa, *De la edad media a nuestros días: estudios de historia literaria* (Madrid: Gredos, 1967) 21, suggests that in the *Romancero,* the *-ra* form is often a simple past tense marker.

[4] R. Lenz, *La oración y sus partes* (Madrid: *RFE,* 1925), comments:

El imperfecto castellano (como el *imparfait* del francés, según Lorck) se dirige a la imaginación, evoca cuadros intuitivos, y así no sólo es adecuado para describir escenas y narrar costumbres, sino que también puede sustituir al pretérito en la narración. (460)

[5] For further discussion, see Labov 375.

[6] The term *phrase structure* refers to the system of rewriting rules which specifies skeletal structures for sentences, denoting a speaker's knowledge of the structure of sentences.

[7] This outline is adapted from Labov 376.

[8] For further discussion, see Louise Mirrer-Singer, "Re-evaluating the *Fronterizo* Ballad: The *Romance de la morilla burlada* as a Pro-Christian Text," *La Corónica* 8.2 (Spring 1985): 157-67.

[9] J. M. Sola-Solé, "En torno al romance de la morilla burlada," *HR* 33 (1965): 136-46. Other important commentaries on the *Romance de la morilla burlada* include Samuel G. Armistead, "¿Existió un romancero de tradición oral entre los moriscos?" *Actas del Coloquio internacional sobre literatura aljamiada y morisca,* ed. Alvaro Galmés de Fuentes (Madrid: Gredos, 1978) 211-36 and María Soledad Carrasco-Urgoiti, *The Moorish Novel: "El Abencerraje" and Pérez de Hita* (New York: Twayne, 1976). Pedro M. Cátedra [García], *Seis pliegos poéticos barceloneses desconocidos c. 1540* (Madrid: El Crotalón, 1983), includes a gloss of the ballad.

[10] "A propos du 'style' de Flaubert," *NRF* 14 (1920): 74.

[11] For example, Szertics uses Proust in his discussion of the "imperfecto narrativo" (102).

[12] Anna Granville-Hatcher, "Tense Usage in the Roland," *SP* 39 (1942): 597-624.

[13] *Tiempo y formas temporales en el "Poema del Cid"* (Madrid: Gredos, 1961) 126.

[14] William Bull, *Time, Tense and the Verb: A Study in Theoretical and Applied Linguistics with Particular Attention to Spanish,* University of California Publications in Linguistics 19 (Berkeley: U of California P, 1960) 34.

[15] "Los romances españoles," *Asomante* 1.1 (1945): 12.

[16] *Algunos caracteres de la cultura española* (Buenos Aires: Espasa-Calpe Argentina, 1942) 21.

[17] Menéndez Pidal, *Romancero hispánico* 1: 77.

[18] Colin Smith and J. Morris, "On 'Physical' Phrases in Old Spanish Epic and Other Texts," *Leeds Philosophical and Literary Society Proceedings* 12.5 (1967), discuss one important extralinguistic feature in particular:

> The "physical" phraseology is used in a remarkably expressive and poetic way, partly because it was a constituent of the speech of the time, partly because the author or minstrel made specifically selective use of it to enhance his performance (by referring a great deal of symbolism to his own body and by exploiting the possibilities of mime). (187)

See also Paul Zumthor, "The Text and the Voice," *NLH* 16.1 (1984): 67-92.

[19] This is a theory which Szertics specifically refutes.

[20] "La 'mezcla de los tiempos narrativos' en el Romancero Viejo," *Romanistisches Jahrbuch* 25 (1974): 278-93, at 281. Sandmann further argues that "la rima es el lugar prosódico en donde las funciones semánticas de la morfología verbal fácilmente se neutralizan" (283). However, he also points out that liberties are often taken with verb forms internal to the verses of a *romance.* This would seem to present a major obstacle to his original argument—an obstacle he attempts to overcome with the statement that the protagonist of a *romance* "puede mezclar con formas lógicas del presente otras del imperfecto sea en posición de rima, sea fuera de ella—si le da la gana" (284-85). Yet Sandmann's own example of two lines from the *Primavera y flor romance,* text 130, suggests that the manipulation of verb forms in the *Romancero* does point to semantic subtleties in the text.

> La reina *parió* en el trono,   la esclava en tierra *paría*
> una hija *parió* la reina,   la esclava un hijo *paría.*

He himself comments, "Los versos en los que se opone la suerte de la reina a la condición de la esclava, arriba citados, ponen de relieve y dan vida a la mezcla de los tiempos narrativos" (289).

An argument somewhat similar in nature to Sandmann's has been presented in a doctoral dissertation by Robert Francis Estelle, "The Interrelationship of Assonance, Verb Forms, and Syntax in the 'Romances Viejos,'" (U of Minnesota, 1970).

[21] "The Folkloristic Pre-Stage of the Spanish Romance 'Conde Arnaldos,'" *HR* 23 (1955): 186.

[22] *BH* 73 (1971): 50-103.

[23] Michèle Débax, "La problématique du narrateur dans le 'Romancero tradicional,'" *Sujet et sujet parlant dans le texte,* Travaux de l'Université de Toulouse-Le Mirail 5 (Toulouse: U de Toulouse Publications, 1977) 43-62.

[24] *Homenaje a Casalduero: crítica y poesía* (Madrid: Gredos, 1972) 151-60.

[25] *Tiempo y formas temporales en el "Poema del Cid."*

[26] Stephen Gilman, rev. of *Tiempo y verbo en el Romancero Viejo,* by Joseph Szertics, *MLN* 83 (1967): 339-43.

[27] Smith, *Spanish Ballads* 5.

[28] William Entwistle, *European Balladry* (Oxford: Clarendon, 1969) 154, is one example.

[29] *WF* 23 (1964): 262-64.

[30] *HR* 46 (1978): 476. See also Benmayor, "Social Determinants in Poetic Transmission, or a Wide-Angle Lens for *Romancero* Scholarship," *RH: Historia* 153-65.

[31] In modern versions, the singer is from the audience.

[32]

. . . he came to the bedside of Lucretia, as she lay asleep, with a drawn sword, and with his left hand pressing down the woman's breast, said: "Be silent, Lucretia; I am Sextus Tarquinius. I have a sword in my hand. You shall die if you utter a word." When the woman, awaking terrified from sleep, saw there was no help, and that impending death was nigh at hand, then Tarquin declared his passion, entreated, mixed threats with entreaties, tried all means to influence the woman's mind. When he saw she was resolved, and uninfluenced even by the fear of death, to the fear of death he added the fear of dishonor, declaring that he would lay a murdered slave naked by her side when dead, so that it should be said that she had been slain in base adultery.

From Titus Livy, *Roman History,* trans. John Henry Freese, Alfred John Church, and William Jackson Brodribb (New York: Appleton, 1904).

[33] Rina Benmayor, *Romances judeo-españoles de Oriente: nueva recolección* (Madrid: Gredos, 1979) 59.

[34] The argument is not constructed on one example alone, for a good number of the versions collected by Benmayor had this interpretation.

[35] See Menéndez Pidal, *Romancero hispánico* 1: 42-43.

[36] Foster 392-94.

[37] Albert B. Lord, *The Singer of Tales* (1960; New York: Atheneum, 1974) 16-17.

Chapter 3: A Sociolinguistic Approach to Narrative Structure in the *Romancero*

[1] Labov studied personal anecdotes told by community members in Harlem, Martha's Vineyard, and Philadelphia, for example. For similar, more recent, studies and for commentary on Labov, see Roger Fowler et al., eds., *Language and Control* (London: Routledge and Kegan Paul, 1979); Gillian Sankoff, *The Social Life of Language* (Philadelphia: U of Pennsylvania P, 1980); David Silverman and Brian Torode, *The Material Word: Some Theories of Language and Its Limits* (London: Routledge and Kegan Paul, 1980).

[2] Labov, ch. 4.

[3] Evaluative language is of course found in written narrative as well as oral texts.

[4] Adapted from Labov 370. This study has found certain overlaps between some of Labov's categories; in particular, the Abstract and Orientation sections.

[5] Mary Louise Pratt, *Toward a Speech Act Theory of Literary Discourse* (Bloomington: Indiana UP, 1977) 73. It should be noted that the notion that literary and nonliterary speech acts share the same catalogue of narrative structures has resulted in something of a polemic. Pratt's work, which is relied on in this study, points to Labov's analysis of oral versions of personal experience as a "corrective" to the literary/ordinary language distinction proposed by many critics of poetry. She argues that the six-part division Labov suggests for analyzing "natural narrative" (Abstract, Orientation, Complicating Action, Evaluation, Result, and Coda) is in near complete conformity with the type of organization observed in literary discourse, using as examples a variety of prose works which, like Labov's narratives, undertake to verbalize experience.

[6] As Labov points out, oral narrators may use other devices (e.g., gestures, expressive phonology) as well as syntactic maneuvers to effect evaluation. The discussion in this study, however, will be largely confined to syntax.

[7] The Resolution of the story of the *morilla burlada* lies outside the text. One may assume that the action of the *romance* led to the violation of Moraima. See J. M. Aguirre, "Moraima y el prisionero: ensayo de interpretación," *Studies of the Spanish and Portuguese Ballad,* ed. N. D. Shergold (London: Tamesis, 1972) 53-72.

[8] Labov frequently asked informants if they had ever been in danger of dying, in order to "overcome the constraints of the face-to-face interview and obtain large bodies of tape-recorded casual speech" (354).

[9] *Literatura, historia, alienación* (Barcelona: Labor, 1976) 25.

[10] Colin Smith, *Spanish Ballads,* writes:

The most striking of ballad openings, and no doubt the most highly evolved, are those in which a speaker begins in direct speech, often a tirade, his name completely unannounced and perhaps not mentioned at all later in the ballad. (32)

[11] Flashback, reordering, and ellipsis are additional examples. Labov notes that these devices fall outside the scope of his study (392).

[12] Two useful papers that address the issue of dialogue in oral speech are Harvey Sacks, "On the Analyzability of Stories by Children," *Directions in Sociolinguistics: The Ethnography of Communication,* ed. J. Gumperz and D. Hymes (New York: Holt, Rinehart and Winston, 1972) 325-45; and J. McH. Sinclair and R. M. Coulthard, *Towards an Analysis of Discourse* (London: Oxford UP, 1975). Sacks's work is interesting in terms of the discussion of evaluation in the *Romancero* because it focuses on the use of certain grammatical items in a conversational exchange which are marked with respect to the relationship between the speakers. Sacks discusses the theoretical and semantic strategies used by speakers in a verbal exchange. He argues that the speakers use a preconditioned knowledge of certain social norms in their discourse in order to recognize as well as achieve desired effects (e.g., gaining the floor, eliciting a response). He also notes that in order to determine the significance of the words used in a verbal exchange, speakers must know something about the lexical items in the competence of the other members of the discourse. Sinclair and Coulthard discuss the analysis of discourse as a means by which the relationship between speakers may be examined. They point to the linguistic actions of the various members of a conversational exchange as an indication of the attitudes each brings to the situation.

[13] The fifteenth-century *juglar,* who may have relied on the singing of the *romances* for his living, would have been constrained in his performance by the frontier attitudes of his interlocutors. It is difficult to imagine such a *juglar* attempting an anti-Christian brand of social interrogation in exchange for his supper.

Chapter 4: A Sociolinguistic Approach to the *Romancero del rey don Pedro*

[1] Colin Smith, *Spanish Ballads,* suggests that the *romances noticieros* "were composed at first by minstrels with the armies and in the service of the nobles, bishops and *adelantados* of Andalusia, and later also by court poets and musicians" (114).

[2] Ramón Menéndez Pidal, *Poesía juglaresca y juglares: aspectos de la historia literaria y cultural de España* (Madrid: Espasa-Calpe, 1942), comments:

Vemos . . . cómo los ministriles y cantores de la corte colaboraban con los juglares de la frontera en interés del elemento oficial. (256-57)

[3] Marie R. Madden, *Political Theory and Law in Medieval Spain* (New York: Fordham UP, 1930) 70. Alfonso XI gave the *Siete Partidas* official approval in the *Cortes* of Alcalá in 1348.

[4] Joseph O'Callaghan, *A History of Medieval Spain* (Ithaca, NY: Cornell UP, 1975) 408.

[5] Legitimacy, in terms of rules of succession, is a concept based not solely on "legitimate" birth. As will be seen in the discussion during the course of this chapter, establishment of legitimacy sometimes extended beyond immediate parentage to an intricate network of kinship and social relations.

[6] Jack Goody, introduction, *Succession to High Office,* ed. Jack Goody (Cambridge: Dept. of Archaeology and Anthropology at Cambridge UP, 1966).

[7] This is the argument of the *romances*; of Pero López de Ayala, whose *Crónica del rey don Pedro* will be discussed in chapter 5 of this study; and of Jean Froissart, *Les chroniques,* ed. J. A. C. Buchon, 3 vols. (Paris, 1867) 1: 503-15; chs. 198-206.

[8] The chronicler, Pero López de Ayala, and his family were among those who suffered from Pedro's rule, according to Luis Suárez Fernández, *El Canciller Ayala y su tiempo* (Vittoria: Dip. Foral de Alava, 1962) n. pag.; ch. 2.

[9] Helen Nader, *The Mendoza Family in the Spanish Renaissance: 1350-1550* (New Brunswick, NJ: Rutgers UP, 1979) 69.

[10] This legitimization was carried out by, among others, Bertrand du Guesclin and his nephew, Sir Olivier. See Froissart 1: 503-15; chs. 198-206.

[11] Madden notes, "The monarchy had become hereditary before the time of the *Partidas* as a natural development of the times" (89), but adds, "hereditary succession did not preclude the idea of choice upon the part of the people" (90).

[12] Yet, as noted by P. E. Russell, *The English Intervention in Spain and Portugal in the Time of Edward III and Richard II* (Oxford: Clarendon, 1955), "in a catalogue of fourteenth-century crimes, Pedro hardly seems to merit the special place which has been allotted him" (17).

[13] *Las Siete Partidas,* in *Los Códigos Españoles* (Madrid, 1847-57), Ley II, Título VI, reads:

> Amar deue el Rey a la Reyna su muger, por tres razones. La primera, porque el e ella por casamiento, segund nuestra Ley, son como vna cosa, de manera que se non pueden partir, sin non por muerte, o por otras cosas ciertas, segund manda Santa Eglesia. La segunda, porque ella solamente deue ser segund derecho, su compañera en los sabores, e en los plazeres: otrosi ella ha de ser su aparcera en los pesares, e en los cuydados. La tercera, porque el linage della ha, o espera auer, que finque en su lugar despues de su muerte. Honrrarla deue otrosi, por tres razones. La primera, porque pues ella es vna cosa con el, quanto mas honrada fuere, tanto es el mas honrrado por ella. La segunda, porque quanto mas la honrrare, tanto aura ella mayor razon, de querer siempre su bien e su honrra. La tercera, porque seyendo ella honrrada, seran los fijos que della ouiere, mas honrrados, e mas nobles. E otrosi la deue guardar por tres razones. La primera, porque non deue auer mas de a ella segund ley, e porende la deue guardar, que la aya a su pro, e que la non pierda. La segunda razon, porque deue ser guardada, es que non diga, nin faga contra ella, nin dexe fazer a otro, ninguna cosa que sea sin razon, ni otro si de carrera a ella, porque lo faga. La tercera razon, porque deue ser mucho guardada, es porque los fijos que della salieren, sean mas ciertos. Onde el Rey, que desta guisa honrrare, e amare, e guardare a su muger, sera el amado, e honrrado, e guardado della, e dara ende buen exemplo a todos los de su tierra.

[14] Menéndez Pidal, *Romancero hispánico* 2: 4.

[15] Smith, *Spanish Ballads* 4.

[16] Robbins Burling, *The Passage of Power: Studies in Political Succession* (New York: Academic, 1974), notes:

> Men who gain power by one set of techniques sometimes promote their ideo-
> logical principles so successfully that they define new conditions for the next
> succession. (7)

[17] This was the first *fronterizo* text, *Cercada tiene a Baeza,* in which King Pedro is referred to as "Pedro Gil, a contemptuous nickname with connotations of bastardy given him by his enemies" (Smith, *Spanish Ballads* 115).

[18] Menéndez y Pelayo, *Antología* 12: 136.

[19] See discussion in this chapter of texts 66 and 66a.

[20] "Quae etiam non multo post lapso tempore, dolore et tristitia obiit, vel secumdum aliquos dolose extitit interempta"—Esteban Baluzio, *Vitae Paparum Avenioniensium* (Paris, 1693) col. 326.

[21] See Entwistle, "The *Romancero*" 309. Although Ruth House Webber, *Formulistic Diction,* doubts Entwistle's contention that more than half of the existing ballad texts were originally composed at the time of the events they report, she states that "certainly . . . these events were recorded in some way soon after their occurrence" (247). Menéndez Pidal, *Romancero hispánico* 2: 4, comments that the *romances noticieros* report "los sucesos de actualidad más interesantes" and refers to the *romances* of the Pedro cycle as "nacidos al calor de las pasiones que encendían la guerra civil entre los dos príncipes hermanos" (5).

[22] See bibliographical information in tables 2-7.

[23] Menéndez Pidal, *Romancero hispánico* 2: 4, comments that relatively few *romances noticieros* have survived the test of time. Russell reasons, "After the triumph of the Trastámarans in 1369, the usurpers' government took administrative measures designed to cause the destruction of as much as possible of the material contained in public and private archives" (18). It is likely that *romances* favorable to Pedro were systematically suppressed when the political situation changed.

[24] Labov 381.

[25] Lenz 458-60.

[26] Szertics, ch. 5.

[27] Szertics, with a stylistic approach, isolates the verb *decir* as a peculiar instance of imperfect usage. Although he notes that this particular verb "cobra a veces sentido itera-tivo y llega incluso a significar 'estaba diciendo' " (122), he sees the imperfect morpheme in *decía* as having a word-specific meaning.

[28] Débax 46.

[29] See note 23 of this chapter.

[30] It is often the case that historical events determine the course of literary history. The establishment of the Inquisition in Spain during the second half of the fifteenth century is an example of such an event. The Inquisition was established in Spain in response to the special problems of a society which viewed religious homogeneity as a central element in its quest for unification and power. This homogeneity, it was believed, could only be achieved through the exclusion of all non-Christian elements from fifteenth-century Catholic Spain.

That the social order in Spain had changed in the fifteenth century to reflect the concerns of a closed community governed by single-minded efforts towards homogeneity is clear from the epitaph on the tombstone of the Catholic rulers:

> Mahometice secte prostratores
> et heretice pervicacie extinctores
> Fernandus Aragonum et Helisabetha Castelle
> vir et uxor unanimes
> Catholici apellati
> marmoreo clauduntur hoc tumulo.

(See Julio Rodríguez-Puértolas, "A Comprehensive View of Medieval Spain," *Américo Castro and the Meaning of Spanish Civilization* [Berkeley: U of California P, 1976] 113-34, at 126.)

That establishing purity of blood was an issue of great importance is clear from such laws as the one which inspired Alonso de Cartagena's 1449 *Defensorium Unitatis Christianae,* the *Sentencia estatuto,* which stated that "no Jews nor those that are from the Jews should ever hold public office, whereby they may bring injury upon Christians" –See Haim Benart, "The *Converso* Community in 15th Century Spain," *The Sephardic Heritage: Essays on the History and Cultural Contribution of the Jews of Spain and Portugal,* ed. R. D. Barnett (New York: KTAV, 1971) 1: 425-56. This law, which actually stemmed from the Church Council of 633, was taken up with great vigor in the fifteenth century. For additional studies of *casticismo* and religious and social intolerance in fifteenth-century Spain, see Arcadio Díaz Quiñones, "Literatura y casta triunfante: el romancero fronterizo," *Sin Nombre* 3 (1973): 8-25; Samuel G. Armistead and Joseph Silverman, "Christian Elements and De-Christianization in the Sephardic *Romancero,*" *Collected Studies in Honour of Américo Castro's Eightieth Year* (Oxford: Lincombe Lodge Research Library, 1965) 36-37; and Dolores Reventlow, "La historia de la Frontera y el romancero fronterizo," diss., U of British Columbia, 1976, 10.

[31] Colin Smith, "On the Ethos of the 'Romancero Viejo,'" *Studies of the Spanish and Portuguese Ballad,* ed. N. D. Shergold (London: Tamesis, 1972), makes the point that "'buen rey' is a sorry sort of cliché, even a sick joke" (15). The reference to the *buen* Maestre in text 67a seems to be of this kind, while *honrado,* repeated twice in text 67, has a different connotation.

[32] See Título II, Ley VI of the *Primera Partida.*

[33] Madden 72. See also A. Ballesteros y Beretta, *Historia de España y su influencia en la historia universal,* 9 vols. (Barcelona: P. Salvat, 1918-41) 3: 433-34.

[34] See Título I, Leyes XIV, XVII, and XVIII of the *Primera Partida.*

[35] Raymond Foulché-Delbosc, *Cancionero castellano del siglo XV,* NBAE 22 (Madrid: Bailly-Bailliere, 1915) 120.

[36] Guillén de Castro y Bellvis, *Obras,* vol. 1, ed. Eduardo Juliá Martínez (Madrid: Imp. de la "Rev. de Archivos, Bibliotecas y Museos," 1925) 12.

[37] See Título II of the *Segunda Partida.*

[38] See discussion in Suárez Fernández, *El canciller Ayala,* ch. 2. Also see note 30 of this chapter.

[39] On prophecy, see Joaquín Gimeno Casalduero, "La profecía medieval en la literatura castellana y su relación con las corrientes proféticas europeas," *NRFH* 20 (1971): 64-89 (especially 82-84) and Edith Random Rogers, *The Perilous Hunt: Symbols in Hispanic and European Balladry* (Lexington: UP of Kentucky, 1980) (especially 23).

[40] Luis Suárez Fernández, "The Atlantic and the Mediterranean Among the Objectives of the House of Trastámara," trans. F. M. López-Morillas, *Spain in the Fifteenth Century,* ed. R. Highfield (New York: Harper and Row, 1972) 51, 59.

[41] Smith, *Spanish Ballads* 4.

[42] See Título II of the *Segunda Partida.*

[43] See Títulos VI-IX of the *Segunda Partida.*

[44] Evaluation, of course, may occur throughout a text. Usually, it is most concentratedly found in one section, called by Labov the Evaluation section.

[45] Entwistle, "The *Romancero*" 322.

[46] MacKay 15-33.

[47] See note 13 of this chapter.

Chapter 5: A Sociolinguistic Approach to the *Crónica del rey don Pedro*

[1] See Robert Scholes and Robert Kellogg, *The Nature of Narrative* (New York: Oxford UP, 1966), for an interesting discussion of the "oral heritage of written narrative."

[2] Scholes and Kellogg state: "The audience shares the narrator's knowledge and values, depending upon him at every point for judgements about the characters and events in the story" (52). Note also Colin Smith, *Spanish Ballads*: "A poem which is to be recited or sung must communicate its sense immediately, since there can be no pause for thought and no turning back the page" (35).

[3] Edward Storer, *Peter the Cruel: The Life of the Notorious Don Pedro of Spain Together with an Account of His Relations with the Famous María de Padilla* (London: John Lane, 1911), relates the following anecdote:

Du Guesclin, the Frenchman who was later to bring ruin to Don Pedro, could barely read and write. When he was besieged in Rennes by the English, he had to give a message sent him by the Duke of Lancaster to another to read for him. (9)

[4] Nader 25.

[5] Nader calls Ayala a "Renaissance historian."

[6] Menéndez y Pelayo, *Antología* 17: 112.

[7] "López de Ayala," in *Historia general de las literaturas hispánicas,* ed. G. Díaz-Plaja, 6 vols. (Barcelona: Barna, 1949) 1: 512.

[8] "Lo hispánico y el erasmismo," *RFE* 4 (1942): 5-6.

[9] Fernán Pérez de Guzmán, *Generaciones y semblanzas,* ed. R. B. Tate (London: Tamesis, 1965):

Fue este don Pero López de Ayala alto de cuerpo e delgado, e de buena presona, onbre de grant discreçión e abtoridad, e de grant consejo ansi de paz como de guerra. Ovo grant lugar açerca de los reyes en cuyo tienpo fue. . . . Fue de muy dulce condiçión e de buena conversaçión e de grant conçiençia, e que temía mucho a Dios. Amó mucho la çiençia, dióse mucho a los libros e estorias, tanto que como quier que él fuese asaz cavallero e de grant discreçión en la plática del mundo, pero naturalmente fue inclinado a las çiençias, e con esto grant parte del tienpo ocupava en el ler e estudiar, non obras de derecho sinon filosofía e estorias. . . . Fizo un buen libro de la caça, que él fue muy caçador. . . . Amó mucho mugeres, más que a tan sabio cavallero como a él se convenía. (15)

[10] *Un prosista anónimo del siglo XIV* (La Laguna, Canary Islands: U La Laguna, 1954). Catalán notes of the earlier *Poema de Alfonso XI*:

Con visión más bien poética que cronística el historiador de Alfonso XI rompe con la técnica de narración descarnada, que le imponía la tradición historiográfica, para captar en todo momento el detalle, inútil a la acción general, pero que da color y dramatismo a lo narrado. (39)

See also Mercedes Vaquero, "El *Poema de Alfonso XI*: ¿Crónica rimada o épica?," diss., Princeton U, 1984, who comments:

The two main goals of the *Poema* [*de Alfonso XI*] are to present the King's political actions in an archetypal and universal manner, and to make propaganda for the kingdom of Alfonso XI. This latter goal is evident in its plain language, its use of verse, its nationalistic sentiment and its sympathy for the lower classes. (iii-iv)

[11] Ayala's immediate successor in royal chronicle writing was Alvar García de Santa María. For further discussion, see Robert Tate, "López de Ayala, Humanist Historian?," *HR* 25 (1957): 157-74.

[12] The edition used here is from *Crónica de los reyes de Castilla,* ed. Cayetano Rosell, BAE 66 (Madrid: Rivadeneyra, 1875-77). For a detailed bibliography of López de Ayala,

see Constance L. Wilkins and Heanon M. Wilkins, "Bibliography of the Works of Pero López de Ayala," *La Corónica* 11.2 (Spring 1983): 336-50. For a discussion of problems relating to Ayala manuscripts, see Jorge N. Ferro, "Observaciones a propósito de la transcripción del Ms. Real Ac. Hist. A-14 (*Crónicas* del Canciller Ayala)," *Incipit* 1 (1981): 67-77.

[13] Nader notes, "In only two instances does Ayala use extraneous material without integrating it into the action" (65).

[14] William J. Entwistle, "The *Romancero*" 316, writes that "proof that the ballad is older than Ayala is . . . incomplete," but later adds "on a balance of probability the original form of this ballad should be attributed to the years 1374-88" (i.e., prior to the composition of the chronicle). Georges E. A. Cirot, "Deux notes sur les rapports entre romances et chroniques," *BH* 30 (1928): 255, also suggests the *romance* as a possible source for Ayala's *clérigo profeta* relation, but claims uncertainty because, in the chronicle, the story is "parfaitement localisé, daté, encadré. . . ." This study finds evidence for the *romance* as Ayala's source for the story on the basis of its similarity to the *romance* versions as well as its uncharacteristic insertion in the chronicle as an anecdote which does not arise out of the logical development of the narrative. It seems that the *clérigo profeta* story, as well as that of the *pastorcico profeta,* were included as afterthoughts by Ayala who perhaps recalled them or heard them sung anew as he put the finishing touches on the chronicle.

[15] See, for example, text 66, discussed in section 4D3 of this study:

>   . . .   mandó matar a la reina
> ese día a un caballero,   pareciéndole acababa
> con su muerte el mal agüero.

[16] Entwistle, "The *Romancero,*" notes:

> what prevents our supposing that the three great murders were already sung in the Trastamaran camps during the lifetime of the unhappy tyrant? They answer perfectly the political needs of the moment . . . the *Romancero del Rey Don Pedro* seems to have been extant before Ayala commenced his chronicle in 1394. (321-22)

[17] Nader 69.

[18] Nader states that Ayala's own family was the intended audience for the *Crónica:*

> Ayala had to take into account one final consideration in excusing his own behavior —the audience to whom he addressed his apology. They were, in fact, his own descendants, the people who benefitted most from Enrique de Trastámara's usurpation of the throne and Ayala's desertion of Pedro. (70)

See also Claudio Sánchez-Albornoz, "El canciller Ayala historiador," *Humanitas* [Tucumán] 1.2 (1953): 13-46; rpt. in *Españoles ante la historia* (Buenos Aires: Losada, 1958) 111-54, who suggests that

> López de Ayala recibió de los Trastámaras el encargo oficioso de escribir las crónicas de los reinados de Pedro I y de sus sucesores. Era tradición de los reyes de

Castilla ese cuidar de que se escribiera la historia de la monarquía. La había iniciado Alfonso el Sabio al ordenar la redacción de la *Crónica General,* la había proseguido Sancho el Bravo, pues por su mandato se concluyó la obra comenzada en la corte de su padre; Alfonso XI había encomendado a Fernán Sánchez de Valladolid que historiara los reinados de sus antepasados; carácter oficioso tiene la Crónica del mismo Alfonso XI; y no puede sorprender que uno de los Trastámaras ordenara a López de Ayala que trazara la historia de su tiempo. (*Españoles* 127-28)

[19] Jeanette Beer, "Medieval Vernacular History: The Medium and Its Public Reception," Literary History and Historical Literature Section, Fifteenth International Congress on Medieval Studies, Kalamazoo, 2 May 1980. The tradition of vernacular history was a tradition of the spoken word. Because the *Crónica* was written in Spanish and not in Latin, it was available to those who might otherwise be considered "unlettered"–in terms of the Middle Ages, unable to read Latin. The ballad audience included this "unlettered" group, as well as the literate Spaniards who, like Ayala, also had heard the texts of the ballads sung. Thus, in many cases, the audience for the ballad and for the *Crónica* would have been one and the same.

[20] Nader notes:

Its popularity among the reading public is attested by the fourteen manuscripts surviving from the fifteenth century and the early and frequent printings in Castile. (61-62)

Evidence of continued readership for the chronicle is its printing history: the *Crónica* was published in Seville in 1495, 1542, and 1549, and in Toledo in 1526–Francesco Branciforti, "Regesto delle opere di Pero López de Ayala," *Saggi e ricerche in memoria di Ettore Li Gotti,* 3 vols., Centro di Studi Filologici e Linguistici Siciliani, Bollettino 6 (Palermo: n.p., 1961) 1: 28-319.

[21] See, for example, Entwistle, "The *Romancero,*" "Prophecy is a rare gift, even among 'pastorcicos' " (311), and Smith, *Spanish Ballads,*

Most of the Castilian ballads, despite their vagueness . . . and their tendency towards sentimentality, preserve a sober down-to-earth attitude. It is pointless to talk of "realism"; but the people are credible and the things that happen to them are feasible. (39-40)

[22] See notes 14 and 16 of this chapter.

[23] On prologues see Margot Ynés Corona De Ley, "The Prologue in Castilian Literature between 1200 and 1400," diss., U of Illinois, 1976. De Ley concludes that

topics related to the issues of veracity and learned authority are found abundantly in [the prologues of thirteenth- through fifteenth-century texts]. The need to preserve knowledge or information which will benefit others is given more than any other as the reason for writing. (252)

[24] Entwistle, "The *Romancero,*" disagrees:

In the absence of more credible sources . . . the ballads are the statement of the opinion generally received among men of authority, and Ayala does not go beyond his rights in relying on them. (314)

[25] In the *romance* versions, the unearthliness of the *pastor* is enhanced by the description of his arrival in the *campos de Jerez*. For example, in text 66a, discussed in section 4D3 of this study, the description is as follows:

> . . .   vio bajar un bulto negro;
> mientras más se acerca el bulto,   más temor le va poniendo
> con el abajarse tanto,   parece llegar al suelo
> delante de su caballo   a cinco pasos de trecho:
> dél salió un pastorcico,   sale llorando y gimiendo,
> la cabeza desgreñada,   revuelto trae el cabello,
> con los pies llenos de abrojos   y el cuerpo lleno de vello;
> en su mano una culebra   y en la otra un puñal sangriento.

[26] Entwistle, "The *Romancero,*" notes:

In asserting that Ayala drew upon poetical sources, we merely bring his work into line with the rest of Peninsular historiography. The father of Spanish chroniclers, the anonymous Monk of Silos, made use of poetical material . . . to eke out his account of the defeat of Rodrigo; and his successor, the author of the *Crónica Najarense,* based part of his work on a Latin poem in hexameters. By Archbishop Rodrigo and Alfonso the Sage the practice was carried over to vernacular history. (313)

Works Consulted

Primary Texts

1. Ballad Collections

Cancionero de romances impreso en Amberes sin año. Ed. Ramón Menéndez Pidal. Madrid: Consejo Superior de Investigaciones Científicas, 1945.

Durán, Agustín. *Romancero general o colección de romances castellanos anteriores al siglo XVIII.* 2nd ed. 2 vols. BAAEE 10 and 16. Madrid, 1851.

Menéndez y Pelayo, Marcelino. *Antología de poetas líricos castellanos.* 14 vols. Madrid: Sucesores de Hernando, 1916-24. Vol. 8. Originally published as *Primeravera y flor de romances,* by F. J. Wolf and C. Hofmann. 2 vols. Berlin, 1856.

Morley, S. G. *Spanish Ballads.* New York: Holt, 1911.

Pérez-Gómez, Antonio. *Romancero del rey don Pedro.* Valencia: La Fonte que Mana y Corre, 1954.

Pliegos poéticos españoles en la Universidad de Praga. 2 vols. Madrid: n.p., 1960.

Pliegos poéticos góticos de la Biblioteca Nacional. 6 vols. Madrid: n.p., 1957-61.

Rodríguez-Moñino, Antonio, ed. *Silva de varios romances.* Barcelona, 1561. Oxford: Dolphin, 1953.

Timoneda, Juan. *Rosas de romances.* Valencia, 1573. Ed. Antonio Rodríguez-Moñino and Daniel Devoto. Oxford: Dolphin, 1963.

2. Chronicles

Alfonso X el Sabio. *Antología de Alfonso X el Sabio.* Ed. Antonio García Solalinde. Madrid: Jiménez-Fraud, 1922.

119

Alfonso X el Sabio. *La primera crónica general.* Ed. Ramón Menéndez Pidal. NBAE 5. Madrid: Bailly-Baillière, 1906.

———. *Las Siete Partidas.* Vols. 2-5 of *Los Códigos Españoles.* Ed. Antonio de San Martín. Madrid, 1872-73.

Froissart, Jean. *Les Chroniques.* Ed. J. A. C. Buchon. 3 vols. Paris, 1867.

López de Ayala, Pero. *Crónica del rey don Pedro. Crónicas de los reyes de Castilla.* Ed. Cayetano Rosell. BAE 66. Madrid: Rivadeneyra, 1875-77.

Secondary Texts

1. History

Branciforti, Francesco. "Regesto delle opere di Pero López de Ayala." *Saggi e ricerche in memoria di Ettore Li Gotti.* 3 vols. Centro di Studi Filologici e Linguistici Siciliani, Bollettino 6. Palermo: n.p., 1962. 1: 289-317.

Caro Baroja, Julio. "Una visión de la vida medieval (Glosa al Canciller Ayala)." *Clavileño* 5.29 (1954): 1-6.

Castro, Américo. "El Canciller Ayala." First publ. as part of "Lo hispánico y el erasmismo." *RFE* 4 (1942): 4-11.

Catalán, Diego. *Un prosista anónimo del siglo XIV: hallazgo, estilo, reconstrucción.* Biblioteca Filológica, Monografías 1. La Laguna, Canary Islands: U La Laguna, 1955.

———, and María Soledad Andrés Castellano de Pliego. "El *Toledano romanzado* y las *Estorias del fecho de los godos* del s. XV." *Estudios dedicados a James Homer Herriott.* Madison: U of Wisconsin P, 1966. 9-102.

Díaz-Plaja, Guillermo. *Historia general de las literaturas hispánicas.* 6 vols. Barcelona: Barna, 1949. Vol. 1.

Floranes, Rafael. *Vida literaria del Canciller Pedro López de Ayala.* Colección de documentos inéditos para la historia de España 19 and 20. Madrid, 1852. Millwood, NY: Krauss, 1966.

Fraker, Charles F. "Gonçalo Martínez de Medina, the Jerónimos, and the Devotio Moderna." *HR* 34 (1966): 197-217.

Gimeno Casalduero, Joaquín. *La imagen del monarca en la Castilla del siglo XIV: Pedro el Cruel, Enrique II y Juan I.* Madrid: Revista de Occidente, 1972.

Hodcroft, F. W., D. G. Pattison, R. D. F. Pring-Mill, and R. W. Truman, eds. *Mediaeval and Renaissance Studies in Honour of P. E. Russell.* London: Oxford UP, 1981.

Meregalli, Franco. *La vida política del Canciller Ayala*. Milan: Cisalpino, 1955.

Mérimée, Prosper. *Histoire de don Pedre 1ᵉʳ Roi de Castille*. Paris: Charpentier, 1961.

Nader, Helen. *The Mendoza Family in the Spanish Renaissance: 1350-1550*. New Brunswick, NJ: Rutgers UP, 1979.

O'Callaghan, Joseph F. *A History of Medieval Spain*. Ithaca, NY: Cornell UP, 1975.

Pérez de Guzmán, Fernán. *Generaciones y semblanzas*. Ed. Robert Brian Tate. London: Tamesis, 1965.

Rebelo, L. de Sousa. "The Idea of Kingship in the Chronicles of Fernão Lopes." *Mediaeval and Renaissance Studies in Honour of P. E. Russell*. Hodcroft 167-79.

Richthofen, Erich von. "The Problem of Fiction Alternating with Historical Documentation in the Cid Epics and the Castilian Chronicles." *RCEH* 6.3 (Spring 1982): 359-76.

Russell, P. E. "Una alianza frustrada. Las bodas de Pedro I de Castilla y Juana Plantagenet." *AEM* 2 (1965): 301-33.

——. *The English Intervention in Spain and Portugal in the Time of Edward III and Richard II*. Oxford: Clarendon, 1955.

Sánchez-Albornoz, Claudio. *Españoles ante la historia*. Buenos Aires: Losada, 1958. 111-54.

Soper, Cherrie Lou. "Pero López de Ayala as Historian and Literary Artist." Diss. U of Kansas, 1967.

Storer, Edward. *Peter the Cruel: The Life of the Notorious Don Pedro of Spain Together with an Account of His Relations with the Famous María de Padilla*. London: John Lane, 1911.

Suárez Fernández, Luis. *El Canciller Ayala y su tiempo: (1332-1407)*. Vitoria: Dip. Foral de Alava, 1962.

——. "The Kingdom of Castile in the Fifteenth Century." *Spain in the Fifteenth Century 1369-1516*. Trans. F. M. López-Morillas. Ed. Roger Highfield. New York: Harper and Row, 1972.

Tate, Robert Brian. "López de Ayala: Humanist Historian?" *HR* 25 (1957): 157-74.

2. Literary, Linguistic, and Historical Theory

Barthes, Roland. "Introduction à l'analyse structurale des récits." *Communications* 8 (1966): 1-27.

Bloch, Marc. *The Historian's Craft*. Manchester, Eng.: Manchester UP, 1954.

Bower, G. H. "Experiments on Story Understanding and Recall." *Quarterly Journal of Experimental Psychology* 28 (1976): 511-34.

Brémond, Claude. *Logic du récit.* Paris: Seuil, 1973.

Bull, William E. *Time, Tense, and the Verb: A Study in Theoretical and Applied Linguistics, with Particular Attention to Spanish.* University of California Publications in Linguistics 19. Berkeley: U of California P, 1960.

Burling, Robbins. *The Passage of Power: Studies in Political Succession.* New York: Academic, 1974.

Collingwood, R. G. *The Idea of History.* Oxford: Clarendon, 1946.

Criado del Val, Manuel. *Sintaxis del verbo español.* 1 vol. Madrid: *RFE,* 1948. Vol. 1.

Eliot, T. S. *The Three Voices of Poetry.* New York: Cambridge UP, 1955.

Faulhaber, Charles. *Latin Rhetorical Theory in Thirteenth and Fourteenth Century Castile.* Berkeley: U of California, 1972.

Fischer, Ernst. *The Necessity of Art.* Trans. Anna Bostock. Baltimore: Penguin, 1963.

Fishman, J. A. "Who Speaks What Language, to Whom and When?" *La Linguistique* 2 (1965): 67-88.

Fowler, Roger, Bob Hodge, Gunther Kress, and Tony Trew, eds. *Language and Control.* London: Routledge and Kegan Paul, 1979.

Goody, Jack, ed. *Succession to High Office.* Cambridge: Dept. of Archaeology and Anthropology at Cambridge UP, 1966.

Greimas, A. J. *Sémantique structurale.* Paris: Larousse, 1966.

Harris, Zelig S. *Discourse Analysis Reprints.* The Hague: Mouton, 1963.

Hauser, Arnold. "Propaganda, Ideology and Art." *Aspects of History and Class Consciousness.* Ed. István Mészáros. New York: Herder and Herder, 1972. 128-51.

———. *The Social History of Art.* 2 vols. New York: Vintage, 1951. Vol. 1.

Hendricks, William O. *Essays on Semiolinguistics and Verbal Art.* The Hague: Mouton, 1973.

Labov, William. *Language in the Inner City.* Philadelphia: U of Pennsylvania P, 1972.

Labov, William, and Joshua Waletzky. "Narrative Analysis: Oral Versions of Personal Experience." *Essays on the Verbal and Visual Arts.* Proceedings of the 1966 Annual Spring Meeting of the American Ethnological Society. Ed. June Helm. Seattle: U of Washington P, 1967. 12-44.

Lakoff, Robin. "Language in Context." *Language* 48.4 (1972): 907-27.

Lapesa, Rafael. *De la edad media a nuestros días: estudios de historia literaria.* Madrid: Gredos, 1967.

Lathrop, Thomas A. *The Evolution of Spanish: An Introduction Historical Grammar.* Newark, DE: Juan de la Cuesta, 1980.

Lenz, R. *La oración y sus partes: estudios de gramática general y castellana.* Madrid: RFE, 1925.

Lukács, Georg. *The Historical Novel.* Trans. Hannah Mitchell and Stanley Mitchell. New York: Humanities, 1965.

Madden, Marie R. *Political Theory and Law in Medieval Spain.* New York: Fordham UP, 1930.

Mandler, Jean M., and Nancy S. Johnson. "Remembrance of Things Parsed: Story Structure and Recall." *Cognitive Psychology* 9 (1977): 111-51.

Ong, Walter. *The Presence of the Word: Some Prologomena for Cultural and Religious History.* New Haven: Yale UP, 1967.

Pêcheux, Michel, and C. Fuchs. "Language, Ideology and Discourse Analysis: An Overview." Trans. and introduction by Eugene W. Holland. *Praxis* 6 (1982): 3-20.

Pratt, Mary Louise. *Toward a Speech Act Theory of Literary Discourse.* Bloomington: Indiana UP, 1977.

Proust, Marcel. "A propos du 'style' de Flaubert." *NRF* 14 (1920): 72-90.

Rodríguez-Puértolas, Julio. *Literatura, historia, alienación.* Barcelona: Labor, 1976.

Sacks, Harvey. "On the Analyzability of Stories by Children." *Directions in Sociolinguistics: The Ethnography of Communication.* Ed. John Gumperz and Dell Hymes. New York: Holt, Rinehart and Winston, 1972. 325-45.

Sankoff, Gillian. *The Social Life of Language.* Philadelphia: U of Pennsylvania P, 1980.

Scholes, Robert, and Robert Kellog. *The Nature of Narrative.* New York: Oxford UP, 1966.

Segre, Cesare. *Le strutture e il tempo: narrazione, poesia, modelli.* Torino: Einaudi, 1974.

Silverman, David, and Brian Torode. *The Material Word: Some Theories of Language and Its Limits.* London: Routledge and Kegan Paul, 1980.

Sinclair, J. McH., and R. M. Coulthard. *Towards an Analysis of Discourse: The English Used by Teachers and Pupils.* London: Oxford UP, 1975.

Stankiewicz, Edward. "Poetics and Verbal Art." *A Perfusion of Signs.* Ed. Thomas Sebeok. Bloomington: Indiana UP, 1977.

Stock, Brian. "Literary Discourse and the Social Historian." *NLH* 8 (1977): 183-94.

Tannen, Deborah, ed. *Spoken and Written Language: Exploring Orality and Literacy.* Norwood, NJ: Ablex, 1982.

Thorndyke, Perry W. "Cognitive Structures in Comprehension and Memory of Narrative Discourse." *Cognitive Psychology* 9 (1977): 77-110.

Turner, Terence S. "Narrative Structure and Mythopoesis." *Arethusa* 10 (1977): 103-63.

3. Oral Literature

Armistead, Samuel G. "Current Trends in *Romancero* Research." *La Corónica* 12.1 (1983): 4.

———. "Epic and Ballad: A Traditionalist Perspective." *Olifant* 8.4 (Summer 1981): 376-88.

———. "Neo-Individualism and the *Romancero.*" *RPh* 33.1 (Aug. 1979): 172-81.

———. "Recent Developments in Judeo-Spanish Ballad Scholarship." *Studies in Jewish Folklore.* Ed. Frank Talmage. Cambridge, MA: Assn. for Jewish Studies, 1980. 21-32.

Armistead, Samuel G., and Joseph H. Silverman. *The Judeo-Spanish Chapbooks of Yacob Abraham Yoná.* Berkeley: U of California P, 1971.

———. "A Judeo-Spanish *Kompla* and Its Greek Counterpart." *WF* 23 (1964): 262-64.

Avalle-Arce, Juan Bautista. "Bernal Francés y su romance." *AEM* 3 (1966): 327-91.

Bénichou, Paul. *Creación poética en el Romancero tradicional.* Madrid: Gredos, 1968.

———. *Romancero judeo-español de Marruecos.* Madrid: Castalia, 1968.

Benmayor, Rina. "A Greek *Tragoúdi* in the Repertoire of a Judeo-Spanish Ballad Singer." *HR* 46 (1978): 475-79.

———. *Romances judeo-españoles de Oriente: nueva recolección.* Madrid: Gredos, 1979.

———. "Social Determinants in Poetic Transmission, or a Wide-Angle Lens for *Romancero* Scholarship." *RH: Historia* 153-65.

Catalán, Diego. "Análisis semiótico de estructuras abiertas: el modelo 'Romancero.'" *RH: Poética* 231-49.

———. "Memoria e invención en el Romancero de tradición oral." *RPh* 24 (1970-71): 1-25, 441-63.

———. "Los modos de producción y 'reproducción' del texto literario y la noción de apertura." *Homenaje a Julio Caro Baroja.* Madrid: Centro de Investigaciones Sociológicas, 1978. 245-70.

Catalán, Diego. *Siete siglos de romancero: historia y poesía.* Madrid: Gredos, 1969.

Catalán, Diego, J. Antonio Cid, Beatriz Mariscal, Flor Salazar, Ana Valenciano, and Sandra Robertson. *Catálogo General del Romancero.* 3 vols. Madrid: S.M.P., 1982-84.

Chevalier, Jean-Claude. "Architecture temporelle du 'Romancero Tradicional.'" *BH* 73 (1971): 50-103.

Cirot, Georges E. A. "Deux notes sur les rapports entre romances et chroniques." *BH* 30 (1928): 250-55.

Débax, Michèle. "La problématique du narrateur dans le 'Romancero tradicional.'" *Sujet et sujet parlant dans le texte.* Travaux de l'Université de Toulouse-Le Mirail 5. Toulouse: U de Toulouse Publications, 1977. 43-62.

Díaz Roig, Mercedes. "Palabra y contexto en la recreación del romancero tradicional." *NRFH* 26 (1977): 460-67.

Entwistle, William J. *European Balladry.* Oxford: Clarendon, 1969.

———. "The *Romancero del Rey Don Pedro* in Ayala and the *Cuarta Crónica General.*" *MLR* 25 (1930): 306-26.

Espinosa, Aurelio. "El Romancero." *Hispania* 12 (1929): 1-32.

Estelle, Robert Francis. "The Interrelationship of Assonance, Verb Forms, and Syntax in the 'Romances Viejos.'" Diss. U of Minnesota, 1970.

Finnegan, Ruth. *Oral Literature in Africa.* London: Clarendon, 1970.

———. *Oral Poetry: Its Nature, Significance, and Social Context.* New York: Cambridge UP, 1977.

Foster, D. W. "A Note on the Rhetorical Structure of the Ballad *Alora la bien cercada.*" *RN* 15 (1973): 392-96.

Garci-Gómez, Miguel. "*Romance* según los textos españoles del Medievo y Prerrenacimiento." *JMRS* 4 (1974): 35-62.

Gilman, Stephen. "On 'Romancero' as a Poetic Language." *Homenaje a Casalduero: crítica y poesía: ofrecido por sus amigos* Madrid: Gredos, 1972. 151-60.

———. *Tiempo y formas temporales en el "Poema del Cid."* Madrid: Gredos, 1961.

———. Rev. of *Tiempo y verbo en el Romancero Viejo,* by Joseph Szertics. *MLN* 83 (1967): 339-43.

González, Aurelio. *Formas y funciones de los principios en el Romancero viejo.* Cuadernos Universitarios 16. México, D. F.: UAM, 1984.

Granville-Hatcher, Anna. "Tense Usage in the Roland." *SP* 39 (1942): 597-624.

Jackson, Barry Bernard. "The Epics of Social Unrest." Diss. U of Oregon, 1977.

Jacobs, Melville. "A Look Ahead in Oral Literature Research." *JAF* 79 (1966): 413-27.

Lord, Albert Bates. *The Singer of Tales.* New York: Atheneum, 1974.

MacKay, Angus. "The Ballad and the Frontier in Late Mediaeval Spain." *BHS* 53 (1976): 15-33.

Menéndez Pidal, Ramón. *Poesía juglaresca y juglares: aspectos de la historia literaria y cultural de España.* Madrid: Espasa-Calpe, 1942.

——. "Poesía popular y romancero." *RFE* 3 (1916): 234-89.

——. "Relatos poéticos en las crónicas medievales." *RFE* 10 (1923): 329-72.

——. *Romancero hispánico (hispano-portugués, americano y sefardí): teoría e historia.* 2nd ed. 2 vols. Madrid: Espasa-Calpe, 1968.

Menéndez y Pelayo, Marcelino. *Tratado de los romances viejos.* Vols. 11 and 12 of *Antología de poetas líricos castellanos desde la formación del idioma hasta nuestros días.* 14 vols. Madrid: Sucesores de Hernando, 1916-24.

Miles, Josephine. "The Language of Ballads." *RPh* 7 (1953): 1-9.

Miletich, John S. "Narrative Style in Spanish and Slavic Traditional Narrative Poetry: Implications for the Study of the Romance Epic." *Olifant* 2.2 (1974): 109-28.

Mirrer-Singer, Louise. "Re-evaluating the *Fronterizo* Ballad: The *Romance de la morilla burlada* as a Pro-Christian Text." *La Corónica* 8.2 (Spring 1985): 157-67.

Reventlow, Dolores. "La historia de la Frontera y el romancero fronterizo." Diss. U of British Columbia, 1976.

Rodríguez, Victor Eloy. "Gestures and 'Physical' Phrases in Medieval Castilian Epic Poetry." Diss. U of Southern California, 1977.

Rodríguez-Puértolas, Julio. *Poesía de protesta en la Edad Media castellana: historia y antología.* Madrid: Gredos, 1968.

Rogers, Edith Random. *The Perilous Hunt: Symbols in Hispanic and European Balladry.* Lexington: UP of Kentucky, 1980.

Sandmann, Manfred. "La 'mezcla de los tiempos narrativos' en el Romancero Viejo." *Romanistisches Jahrbuch* 25 (1974): 278-93.

Sheub, Harold. "Body and Image in Oral Narrative Performance." *NLH* 8 (1977): 245-367.

Smith, Colin. *Spanish Ballads.* 1964. Oxford: Pergamon, 1971.

Smith, Colin. "On the Ethos of the 'Romancero Viejo.'" *Studies of the Spanish and Portuguese Ballad.* Ed. N. D. Shergold. London: Tamesis, 1972. 5-24.

Smith, Colin, and J. Morris. "On 'Physical' Phrases in Old Spanish Epic and Other Texts." *Leeds Philosophical and Literary Society Proceedings* 12.5 (1967): 129-90.

Solá-Solé, Josep M. "En torno al romance de la morilla burlada (Moraima)." *HR* 33 (1965): 136-46.

Spitzer, Leo. "The Folkloristic Pre-Stage of the Spanish Romance 'Conde Arnaldos.'" *HR* 23 (1955): 173-87.

———. "Los romances españoles." *Asomante* 1.1 (1945): 7-29.

Szertics, Joseph. "Observaciones sobre algunas funciones estilísticas del pretérito indefinido en el Romancero Viejo." *ExTL* 2 (1974): 189-97.

———. *Tiempo y verbo en el Romancero Viejo.* Madrid: Gredos, 1967.

Vossler, Karl. "Carta española a Hugo von Hofmannsthal." *Algunos caracteres de la literatura española.* Buenos Aires: Espasa-Calpe Argentina, 1942. 9-47.

Webber, Ruth House. *Formulistic Diction in the Spanish Ballad.* Berkeley: U of California P, 1951.

———. "Lenguaje tradicional: epopeya y romancero." *Actas del Sexto Congreso Internacional de Hispanistas.* Toronto: U of Toronto P, 1980. 779-82.

———. "Prologomena to the Study of the Narrative Structure of the Hispanic Ballad." *Ballads and Ballad Research.* Selected papers of the International Conference on Nordic and Anglo-American Ballad Research. Seattle: U of Washington P, 1978. 221-30.

Wilson, Edward Meryon. *Tragic Themes in Spanish Ballads.* London: Hispanic and Luso-Brazilian Councils, 1958.

Zumthor, Paul. "The Text and the Voice." *NLH* 16.1 (1984): 67-92.

4. Other Works

Castro y Bellvis, Guillén de. *Obras.* Vol. 1. Ed. Eduardo Juliá Martínez. Madrid: Imp. de la "Rev. de Archivos, Bibliotecas y Museos," 1925.

De Ley, Margo Ynés Corona. "The Prologue in Castilian Literature between 1200 and 1400." Diss. U of Illinois, 1976.

Foulché-Delbosc, Raymond. *Cancionero castellano del siglo XV.* NBAE 22. Madrid: Bailly-Baillière, 1915.

Gimeno Casalduero, Joaquín. "La profecía medieval en la literatura castellana y su relación con las corrientes proféticas europeas." *NRFH* 20 (1971): 64-89.

Lomba y Pedraja, José R. "El rey don Pedro en el teatro." *Homenaje a Menéndez y Pelayo en el año vigésimo de su profesoriado.* 2 vols. Madrid, 1899. 2: 257-339.

Menéndez y Pelayo, Marcelino. *Estudios sobre el teatro de Lope de Vega.* 6 vols. Santander: Aldus, S. A. de Artes Gráficas, 1949. Vol. 4.

Molho, Michael. *Usos y costumbres de los sefardíes de Salónica.* Trans. F. Pérez Castro. Madrid: Consejo Superior de Investigaciones Científicas, Instituto Arias Montano, 1950.

Vaquero, Mercedes. "El *Poema de Alfonso XI*: ¿Crónica rimada o épica?" Diss. Princeton U, 1984.

In the PURDUE UNIVERSITY MONOGRAPHS IN ROMANCE LANGUAGES series the following monographs have been published thus far:

1. John R. Beverley: *Aspects of Góngora's "Soledades"*.
   Amsterdam, 1980. xiv, 139 pp. Bound.

2. Robert Francis Cook: *"Chanson d'Antioche," chanson de geste: Le Cycle de la Croisade est-il épique?*
   Amsterdam, 1980. viii, 107 pp. Bound.

3. Sandy Petrey: *History in the Text: "Quatrevingt-Treize" and the French Revolution.*
   Amsterdam, 1980. viii, 129 pp. Bound.

4. Walter Kasell: *Marcel Proust and the Strategy of Reading.*
   Amsterdam, 1980. x, 125 pp. Bound.

5. Inés Azar: *Discurso retórico y mundo pastoral en la "Egloga segunda" de Garcilaso.*
   Amsterdam, 1981. x, 171 pp. Bound.

6. Roy Armes: *The Films of Alain Robbe-Grillet.*
   Amsterdam, 1981. x, 216 pp. Bound.

7. *Le "Galien" de Cheltenham,* edited by David M. Dougherty and & Eugene B. Barnes.
   Amsterdam, 1981. xxxvi, 203 pp. Bound.

8. Ana Hernández de Castillo: *Keats, Poe, and the Shaping of Cortázar's Mythopoesis.*
   Amsterdam, 1981. xii, 135 pp. Bound.

9. Carlos Albarracín-Sarmiento: *Estructura del* "Martín Fierro".
   Amsterdam, 1981. xx, 336 pp. Bound.

10. C. George Peale et al. (eds.): *Antigüedad y actualidad de Luis Vélez de Guevara: Estudios críticos.*
    Amsterdam, 1983. xii, 298 pp. Bound.

11. David Jonathan Hildner: *Reason and the Passions in the "Comedias" of Calderón.*
    Amsterdam, 1982. xii, 119 pp. Bound.

12. Floyd Merrell: *Pararealities: The Nature of Our Fictions and How We Know Them.*
    Amsterdam, 1983. xii, 170 pp. Bound.

13. Richard E. Goodkin: *The Symbolist Home and the Tragic Home: Mallarmé and Oedipus.*
    Amsterdam, 1984. xvi, 203 pp. Paperbound.

14. Philip Walker: *"Germinal" and Zola's Philosophical and Religious Thought.*
    Amsterdam, 1984. xii, 157 pp. Paperbound.

15. Claire-Lise Tondeur: *Gustave Flaubert, critique: Thèmes et structures.*
    Amsterdam, 1984. xiv, 119 pp. Paperbound.

16. Carlos Feal: *En nombre de don Juan (Estructura de un mito literario).*
    Amsterdam, 1984. x, 175 pp. Paperbound.

17. Robert Archer: *The Pervasive Image. The Role of Analogy in the Poetry of Ausiàs March.*
    Amsterdam, 1985. xi, 220 pp. Paperbound.

18. Diana Sorensen Goodrich: *The Reader and the Text: Interpretative Strategies for Latin American Literatures.* Amsterdam, 1986. xi, 150 pp. Paperbound.

19. Lida Aronne-Amestoy: *Utopía, Paraíso e Historia: Inscripciones del mito en García Márquez, Rulfo y Cortázar.* Amsterdam, 1986. xi, 167 pp. Paperbound.

20. Louise Mirrer-Singer: *The Language of Evaluation: A Sociolinguistic Approach to the Story of Pedro el Cruel in Ballad and Chronicle.*
    Amsterdam, 1986. xi, 130 pp. Paperbound.

21. Jo Ann Marie Recker: *"Appelle-moi 'Pierrot'": Wit and Irony in the "Lettres" of Madame de Sévigné.*
    Amsterdam, 1986. ix, 128 pp. Paperbound.

22. J.H. Matthews: *André Breton: Sketch for an Early Portrait.*
    Amsterdam, 1986. xii, 176 pp. Paperbound.